RETOLD TALES SERIES

RETOLD AMERICAN CLASSICS
   VOLUME 1

RETOLD AMERICAN CLASSICS
   VOLUME 2

RETOLD BRITISH CLASSICS

RETOLD WORLD CLASSICS

RETOLD CLASSIC MYTHS
   VOLUME 1

RETOLD CLASSIC MYTHS
   VOLUME 2

RETOLD AMERICAN CLASSIC NONFICTION

The Perfection Form Company, Logan, Iowa 51546

CONTRIBUTING
WRITERS

William S. E. Coleman, Jr.
M.A.T. English and Education
Educational Writer

Judy Lawson
Ph.D. English
Educational Writer

RETOLD TALES SERIES

**RETOLD
AMERICAN
CLASSIC
NONFICTION**

THE PERFECTION FORM COMPANY

Editor-in-Chief:
Kathleen Myers

Editor:
Beth Obermiller

Cover Art: Don Tate
Book Design: Dea Marks
Inside Illustration: Don Tate

TABLE
OF CONTENTS

WELCOME TO THE RETOLD AMERICAN CLASSIC NONFICTION

Give me liberty or give me death." "To be great is to be misunderstood." "A majority of one."

These phrases, spoken and written by great Americans, have worked their way into our vocabulary. They belong to the great tradition of nonfiction classics.

We call something a classic when it is so well loved that it is saved and passed down to new generations. Classics have been around for a long time, but they're not dusty or out of date. That's because they are brought back to life by each new person who reads and enjoys them.

The *Retold American Classic Nonfiction* selections are speeches, essays, and parts of autobiographies that continue to influence today. The selections offer exciting, amusing, frightening, and striking ideas. They are works that people continue to think about, debate, and share.

RETOLD UPDATE

This book presents a collection of eight adapted classics. All the unique, powerful details of the original selections are here. But in the Retold versions, long sentences and paragraphs have been split up.

In addition, a word list has been added at the beginning of each story to make reading easier. Each word defined on that list is printed in dark type within the selection. If you forget the meaning of a word while you're reading, just check the list to review the definition.

You'll also see footnotes at the bottom of some pages. These notes identify people or places as well as explain ideas or words.

Finally, at the end of each tale you'll find a little information about the author. These revealing and sometimes amusing facts will give you insight into a writer's life and work.

One last word. Some of these pieces are just sections from a larger work. If you enjoy what you read here, we encourage you to go to the original versions to get more of the authors' ideas.

Now on to the selections. Remember, when you read this book, you bring each selection back to life in today's world. We hope you'll discover why these pieces have earned the right to be called classics.

SINNERS IN THE HANDS OF AN ANGRY GOD
JONATHAN EDWARDS

VOCABULARY PREVIEW

Below is a list of words that appear in the story. Read the list and get to know the words before you start the story.

abhors—hates
aliens—strangers; outsiders
congregation—group or gathering of church members
divine—godly; heavenly
elect—selected or chosen people
flattering—deceiving or misleading
infinitely—endlessly; greatly
lest—for fear that
loathsome—disgusting; horrid
obligation—duty; responsibility
omnipotent—almighty; unlimited
perishing—dying
pleasure—wish; desire
renouncing—rejecting; giving up (a bad habit)
salvation—the act of being saved (from sin or punishment); rescue
singe—burn slightly
slumber—nap; sleep
unconverted—not persuaded to believe or adopt a new religion; not "reborn"
vengeance—an act done to get even; revenge
wrath—violent anger; rage

SINNERS IN THE HANDS OF AN ANGRY GOD[1]

JONATHAN EDWARDS

Are we good because we long to do the right thing?

Or are we good because we fear punishment?

To Jonathan Edwards, fear was a more powerful emotion. And in this sermon, he describes a God frightening enough to scare listeners straight into heaven.

[1]This is a selection from a sermon Edwards gave in 1741. According to Edwards' religion, God had long ago determined who would be saved and who would be damned. And nothing could save a person who was fated to be damned.

The **wrath** of God is like great waters that are dammed for the present. They increase more and more and rise higher and higher until an outlet is given. And the longer the stream is stopped, the more rapid and mighty it is when it is let loose.

'Tis[2] true that judgment against your evil deeds has not been carried out so far. The floods of God's **vengeance** have been withheld.

But your guilt in the meantime is constantly increasing. You are every day storing up more of his wrath. The waters are continually rising and growing more and more mighty.

Nothing but the **pleasure** of God holds back the waters that are unwilling to be stopped and press to go forward. What if God should withdraw his hand from the floodgate? It would immediately fly open. The fiery floods of God's fierceness and wrath would rush forth with terrible fury. They would come upon you with **omnipotent** power.

No matter if your strength were ten thousand times greater than it is. Yea,[3] no matter if it were ten thousand times greater than that of the strongest, sturdiest devil in Hell. It would be nothing to withstand or survive God's wrath.

The bow of God's wrath is bent. The arrow stands ready on the bowstring. Justice points the arrow at your heart and strains the bow.

What keeps the arrow one moment from being made drunk with your blood? Nothing but the pleasure of God—an angry God, without any promise or **obligation**.

Thus are all of you who have never had a great change of heart. You who have never felt the mighty power of God's spirit touch your souls. You who were never born again and made new creatures.[4] You who were never raised from being dead in sin to a state of new light and life.

No matter if you have reformed your life in many things. No matter if you may have had religious feelings. No matter if you may keep up a form of religion in your families

---

[2]An old expression for "it's."
[3]An old expression for "yes" or "truly."
[4]To be "born again" means to accept Christ as one's savior or deliverer.

and households and the house of God. No matter if you may be strict about following the rules of that religion.

Nevertheless, you are in the hands of an angry God. 'Tis nothing but his pleasure that keeps you from being swallowed up this moment in everlasting destruction.

You may be unconvinced by the truth of what you hear. But by and by, you will be fully convinced of it.

Those who were once in your situation see that this proved true for them. Destruction came suddenly upon most of them when they never expected it. And it came while they were saying *peace and safety*. Now they see that those things they depended on for peace and safety were nothing but thin air and empty shadows.

God holds you over the pit of Hell. He holds you like someone holds a spider or some **loathsome** insect over a fire. He **abhors** you and is dreadfully angered. His wrath towards you burns like fire. He looks upon you as worthy of nothing else but to be cast into the fire.

His eyes are purer than to bear to have you in his sight. You are ten thousand times more hateful in his eyes than the most poisonous snake. You have offended him **infinitely** more than ever a stubborn traitor did his prince.

And yet, 'tis nothing but his hand that holds you from falling into the fire at any moment.

'Tis no other reason why you did not go to Hell last night. 'Tis no other reason why you were allowed to wake again in this world after you closed your eyes to sleep. 'Tis no other reason you have not dropped into Hell since you arose this morning. The only reason is that God's hand held you up.

'Tis no other reason why you have not gone to Hell since you sat down here in the house of God. You have annoyed his pure eyes by attending his solemn worship in a sinful, wicked manner. Yea, there is no other reason why you don't this very moment drop down into Hell.

O sinner! Consider the fearful danger you are in. 'Tis a great furnace of wrath you are held over in the hand of God.

'Tis a wide and bottomless pit, full of the fire of wrath. And God is as angered and enraged against you as against many of the damned in Hell.

You hang by a slender thread. The flames of **divine** wrath flash about it. They are ready every moment to **singe** it and burn it through.

You have no friend to save you. You have nothing to lay hold of to save yourself. Nothing will keep off the flames of wrath. Nothing of your own, nothing you ever have done, nothing you can do will save you. Nothing can persuade God to spare you one moment.

***

And what of many in this **congregation** now hearing this sermon? There is reason to think that they will feel this very misery I describe to the end of time.

We know not who they are. We know not in what seats they sit or what thoughts they now have. It may be they are now at ease. They may hear all these things without much disturbance. They are now **flattering** themselves that they are not such people. They are promising themselves that they shall escape.

How many in this congregation will feel this misery? Suppose we knew there were one person and only one. What an awful thing would it be to think of! If we knew who it was, what an awful sight would it be to see such a person! How might all the rest of the congregation raise a sad and bitter cry over him!

But alas![5] Instead of one, how many is it who are likely to remember this sermon in Hell? It would be a wonder if some who are now present will not be in Hell in a very short time. Perhaps before this year is out. And it would be no wonder if some person sitting here—quiet and secure—should be there before tomorrow morning.

Those of you who shall live out your natural lives shall

[5]An expression of sadness or sorrow.

keep out of Hell longest. But even you will be there in a little time! Your damnation doesn't **slumber**. It will come swiftly and very suddenly upon many of you.

You have reason to wonder that you are not already in Hell. 'Tis doubtless the case of some that you have seen and known before. They may not even have deserved Hell more than you. And once they may have appeared as likely to have been alive today as you.

But now their case is past all hope. They are crying in extreme misery and pure despair.

But here you are in the land of the living and the house of God. You have an opportunity to obtain **salvation**. Think of those poor, damned, helpless souls. What would they give for one day's opportunity such as you now enjoy!

And now you have an extraordinary opportunity. It is a day in which Christ has flung the door of mercy wide open.[6] He stands in the door calling and crying out with a loud voice to poor sinners.

It is a day in which many are flocking to him. They press into the kingdom of God. Many are coming daily from the east, west, north, and south. Many, who were very lately in the same miserable condition as you, are now in a happy state. Their hearts are filled with love for Christ. He has loved them and washed them from their sins in his own blood. Now they rejoice in hope of the glory of God.

How awful is it to be left behind at such a day! To see so many others feasting while you are starving and **perishing**! To see so many rejoicing and singing because their hearts are joyful! But you have cause to mourn for the sorrow in your heart. You have reason to howl for the pain in your spirit!

How can you rest one moment in such a condition? Are not your souls as precious as the souls of the people of Suffield?[7] There they are flocking to Christ from day to day.

---

[6]Christians believe that Christ, the son of God, died to save humans from their sins. In Edwards' sermon, he is described as forgiving and loving. Thus, he sharply contrasts with the wrathful, unforgiving God.

[7]A town close to Enfield, Connecticut. Edwards gave this sermon at Enfield.

Are there many here who have lived *long* in the world and are still not born again? Are they not **aliens** from Israel[8] who have done nothing since birth except store up wrath against the day of wrath?[9]

Oh sirs, your case is extremely dangerous. Your guilt and hardness of heart is extremely great. Don't you see how generally persons of your age are passed over and left? Even on this remarkable and wonderful day when God is handing out mercy?

You had better consider yourselves and wake thoroughly out of sleep. You cannot bear the fierceness and wrath of the infinite God.

And what of you who are *young men* and *young women?* Will you neglect this precious chance that you now enjoy? So many others of your age are **renouncing** all youthful follies and flocking to Christ.

You, especially, have now an extraordinary opportunity. But you must not neglect it. Otherwise, you will be like those who spent their precious youth in sin. Now they are in a dreadful state of blindness and hardness.

And what of you *children* that are **unconverted**? Don't you know that you are going down to Hell? There you will bear the dreadful wrath of God, who is angry with you every day and every night.

Will you be content to be children of the Devil? So many other children in the land are converted. They have become the holy and happy children of the King of kings.[10]

Every one of you who has not joined Christ now hangs over the pit of Hell. You may be old men and women, middle-aged, young people, or little children. But all of you should now listen to the loud calls of God's word and his divine plan.

This year of the Lord is a day of great favor to some.

---

[8]Here "Israel" might be read to mean "heaven."
[9]The "day of wrath" is another term for the Last Judgment. On this day, God is supposed to decide whether each person will be saved or damned for all time.
[10]"King of kings" is another name for Christ.

But it will doubtless be a day of remarkable vengeance to others. Men's hearts harden and their guilt increases greatly on such a day as this if they neglect their souls. Never was there so great a danger that such persons will let hardness of heart and blindness of mind overcome them.

God seems now to be hastily gathering in his **elect** in all parts of the land. Probably more adults than ever shall be saved shortly. It will be like it was in the Apostles' days when there was a great outpouring of the Spirit upon the Jews.[11] The elect will be saved. The rest will be blinded.

If this should be the case with you, you will curse this day to the end of time. You will curse the day that you were born to see such an outpouring of God's Spirit. You will wish that you had died and gone to Hell before you had seen it.

Now, undoubtedly, it is as it was in the days of John the Baptist.[12] In an extraordinary manner, the axe is laid at the root of the trees. Every tree that does not bring forth good fruit may be cut down and cast into the fire.

Therefore, let everyone who is not with Christ awaken and fly from the wrath to come. The wrath of Almighty God is now undoubtedly hanging over a great part of this congregation. Let everyone fly out of Sodom.[13] "Haste and escape for your lives. Look not behind you. Escape to the mountain, **lest** you be destroyed."

[11]The Apostles were Christ's followers. After his death, the Holy Spirit (the spirit of God) visited them. The day of the visit—called Pentecost—is still celebrated seven Sundays after Easter.

[12]John the Baptist was a prophet who foretold the coming of Christ.

[13]Sodom, a biblical city, was destroyed for its wickedness. The closing quotation is from the Bible.

INSIGHTS INTO
JONATHAN EDWARDS

(1703-1758)

Edwards was the fifth child and only son in a family of eleven children. Edwards himself went one better. He and his wife had twelve children—one child every two years.

Edwards was educated at home in the family parlor. The teacher was his father, and his classmates were his sisters and friends.

Though the schoolhouse might seem odd to us, it didn't keep Edwards from learning. He knew some Latin by the time he was six. Hebrew and Greek came somewhat later.

By the age of eleven or twelve, Edwards was producing long, well-researched papers. His essay "Of Insects" was a complex report on the field spider's habits. The paper was based on his own research.

When Edwards was twelve, he was ready for college. Four years later, he graduated from Yale University—at the head of his class.

Edwards was following in his father's footsteps by becoming a minister. In fact, Edwards came from a long line of ministers.

Edwards found his calling very early in life. As a child, he prayed five times a day in secret. He even built a booth in a deep swamp. There he delivered sermons to his friends.

These youthful religious feelings deepened as Edwards grew. By the time he was eighteen, he had taken his first minister's post.

Life at the Edwards home was simple. The family ate meat once a day. Breakfast and supper consisted of bread and milk. The only wine they drank was that left over from religious services. Chocolate, coffee, and rum were viewed as luxuries.

Edwards' life was not only simple but exhausting. He rose early in the morning, between 4:00 and 5:00. Then he generally spent thirteen hours studying. With his great thirst for knowledge, Edwards read all the books he could get his hands on in all subject areas.

Edwards enjoyed horseback riding. He would usually ride two or three miles after dinner to some lonely grove. There he would dismount and walk awhile.

Edwards always carried paper when he walked. That way, he could jot down his ideas while strolling. Then, like a living bulletin board, he would pin the sheets to his coat. Once he reached home, the papers helped inspire his essays and sermons.

Though Edwards proved to be popular in the pulpit, he was aloof in person. He disliked small talk. And he never laughed, seldom smiled.

But Edwards loved children. He got along with them better than with adults.

Edwards is credited with starting the Great Awakening. During this time, many people in Massachusetts became deeply and wildly concerned with religion.

With his fiery sermons, Edwards whipped his listeners in Northampton into a frenzy. People grew so excited, they threw fits and declared they were saved from the devil.

Religion became the number-one concern in Edwards' town. And the fever spread to nearby towns and villages. It is reported that one minister gave a rousing sermon that lasted twenty-four hours!

continued

Finally the Great Awakening got out of hand. Many people grew crazy with fear that they may not have been saved. A few, including Edwards' uncle, became so wild that they killed themselves.

When the frenzy at last died down, Edwards' popularity also declined. People began to resent Edwards and thought he acted too much like God. They didn't like the way he declared that certain people hadn't really been converted.

Then Edwards decided to refuse church membership to those who couldn't prove they had been converted. That was the last straw. By a large majority, the people voted to dismiss Edwards.

But Northampton wasn't yet finished with Edwards. It took four years for the town to find another minister. So the embarrassed town was forced to hire Edwards week by week to preach. Edwards accepted this offer for six months only because he needed money.

This experience didn't cool Edwards' religious zeal. But with his bad name, Edwards knew not many towns would take him on as minister. Yet money was running out, and Edwards had to find work quickly.

At last an opening came. Edwards was asked to serve as pastor to an Indian settlement in Massachusetts.

Edwards not only preached to the Indians. He also came up with a better way of teaching them English. In addition, Edwards wrote several of his major works during his six years at this post.

Though he was a devoted minister, Edwards nearly gave it up for a new career. In 1758, he reluctantly agreed to become president of the new college at Princeton. But his presidency ended scarcely before it had begun. Following his arrival at Princeton, Edwards died after receiving a shot to protect him from smallpox.

Other works by Edwards
 Freedom of the Will, treatise
 "God Glorified in Man's Dependence," sermon
 The Great Christian Doctrine of Original Sin
  Defended, treatise
 "Nature of True Virtue," essay
 "Personal Narrative," narrative
 A Treatise Concerning Religious Affections,
  treatise

"GIVE ME LIBERTY"
PATRICK HENRY

VOCABULARY PREVIEW

Below is a list of words that appear in the story. Read the list and get to know the words before you start the story.

adversary—foe; enemy
arduous—difficult; hard to do
avert—avoid or prevent; turn aside
basely—shamefully; cowardly
delusive—misleading
destinies—fortunes; futures
illusions—false ideas or dreams
inevitable—impossible to avoid
invincible—unable to be conquered; unbeatable
just—fair
petition—formal request or plea
reconciliation—the restoring of friendship or peace;
    making up
remonstrated—protested; objected
revere—to honor; to love and respect
sentiments—feelings
subjugation—slavery or enslavement
submission—act of giving up or in
supplication—prayer or request
tyrannical—powerful in an unjust way; unjust
vigilant—watchful; alert

GIVE ME LIBERTY

PATRICK HENRY

Is war ever the right answer?
For Patrick Henry, it was the only
answer when America's liberty was
at stake.

Mr. President : No man thinks
more highly than I do of the patriotism and
abilities of the very worthy gentlemen who just
spoke.[1] But different men often see the same
subject in different ways. So I hope I will not
seem disrespectful to those gentlemen. However,
I hold opinions opposite to theirs. And I speak
forth my **sentiments** freely and without holding
back.

---

[1]Henry gave this speech before a convention in Virginia in 1775. The aim of the
convention was to discuss the increase in British troops in the American colonies.
After proposing that Virginia prepare for war, Henry gave this speech.

This is no time for ceremony. The question we are debating is one of great importance to this country. For my own part, I consider it nothing less than a question of freedom or slavery. And the openness of the debate ought to be equal to its subject. Only in this way can we hope to arrive at truth and fulfill our great duty to God and our country.

Should I keep back my opinions at this time for fear of offending someone? If I did, I would consider myself guilty of treason toward my country. I would also be disloyal toward the Majesty of Heaven,[2] whom I **revere** above all earthly kings.

Mr. President, it is natural for man to give in to **illusions** of hope. We tend to shut our eyes against a painful truth. We listen to the song of that siren[3] till she changes us into beasts.

Is this the behavior of wise men? Men who are involved in a great and **arduous** struggle for liberty? Are we like those who refuse to see or hear things that concern our earthly welfare?

For my part, I am willing to know the whole truth, whatever pain of spirit it costs me. I want to know the worst and to prepare for it.

I have but one lamp by which my feet are guided. That is the lamp of experience. I know of no way of judging the future but by the past.

So judging by the past, let us examine the behavior of the British government for the last ten years. And I wish to know how that behavior gives hope to the gentlemen of the house. Is it that crafty smile with which the British lately received our **petition**?[4]

Trust it not, sir. It will prove a trap for your feet. Do

---

[2]"The Majesty of Heaven" means God.

[3]In Greek myths, sirens were creatures with women's heads and birds' bodies. Sailors who heard their song were driven mad and crashed their ships.

[4]Henry is referring to a request by the American colonies for more freedom and justice. The British government ignored the request.

not let yourselves be betrayed with a kiss.[5]

Ask yourselves a question about this kind treatment of our petition. Does it match those preparations for war which cover our waters and darken our land? Are fleets and armies needed for an act of love and **reconciliation**? Have we seemed so unwilling to reconcile that they must call in force to win back our love?

Let us not deceive ourselves, sir. These are the tools of war and **subjugation**. These are the last arguments which kings use.

Sir, I ask the gentlemen this question. What means this show of arms if not to force us to **submission**? Can the gentlemen offer any other possible motive for it? Has Great Britain any enemy in these parts that calls for all these navies and armies?

No, sir, she has none. They are meant for us. They can be meant for no other. They are sent over to bind us with chains which the British have been making for a long time.

And what do we have to fight them with? Shall we try argument? Sir, we have been trying that for the last ten years.

Do we have anything new to offer on the subject? Nothing. We have held the subject up in every light. But it has all been in vain.

Shall we try pleading and humble **supplication**? What terms shall we find that we have not already exhausted? I beg you, sir, let us not deceive ourselves any longer.

Sir, we have done everything possible to **avert** the storm which is now coming on. We have petitioned. We have **remonstrated**. We have supplicated. We have knelt before the throne and begged the king to stop the **tyrannical** hands of the government.

But our petitions have been ignored. Our remonstrances have produced more violence and insult. Our supplications

---

[5]In the Bible, Judas betrayed Jesus to Roman soldiers by kissing him. Thus, the soldiers knew which man to arrest.

have been brushed aside. And we have been pushed away with contempt from the foot of the throne!

After all this, it is useless for us to hold on to foolish hopes of peace and reconciliation. There is no longer any room for hope.

Do we wish to be free? Do we intend to save those priceless privileges for which we have been fighting so long? Do we intend not to **basely** abandon our long noble struggle? A struggle we pledged to continue until we gained our glorious goal?

If so, we must fight! I repeat it, sir, we must fight! A call to arms to the God of armies is all that we have left!

They tell us, sir, that we are weak. They say we are unable to deal with so strong an **adversary**.

But when shall we be stronger? Will it be the next week or the next year? Will it be when we are totally disarmed and a British guard is in every house?

Shall we gather strength by uncertainty and lack of action? Shall we resist by lying on our backs and hugging **delusive** hopes until our enemies tie us hand and foot?

Sir, we are not weak if we properly use those means which God has placed in our power. Think of what three million people armed in the holy cause of liberty can do. And in such a country as this, we would be **invincible** against any enemy forces.

Besides, sir, we shall not fight our battles alone. There is a **just** God who rules over the **destinies** of nations. That God will gather friends to fight our battles for us.

The battle, sir, is not won just by the strong. The **vigilant**, the active, and the brave will be the winners.

Besides, sir, we have no choice. Even if we were base enough to desire it, it is now too late to back out of the contest. There is no retreat except to submission and slavery! Our chains are made! Their clanging may be heard on the plains of Boston!

The war is **inevitable**! So let it come! I repeat it, sir, let it come!

It is useless, sir, to try to make this matter seem less serious. The gentlemen may cry, "Peace, peace."

But there is no peace. The war has actually begun! The next wind that sweeps from the North[6] will bring to our ears the echoes of clashing weapons! Our brothers are already on the battlefield! Why do we stand here idle?

What is it that the gentlemen wish? What would they have? Is life so dear or peace so sweet that we should buy them at the price of chains and slavery?

Forbid it, Almighty God! I know not what course others may take. But as for me, give me liberty or give me death!

[6]Some colonists in Massachusetts (the North) were already fighting the British.

INSIGHTS INTO
PATRICK HENRY

(1736-1799)

Looking at Patrick Henry's childhood, you might not guess he would become known for cleverness. He had very little schooling. In fact, his education was mostly limited to what his father taught him at home. Hunting, fishing, dancing, and mischief interested him more than books.

It took Henry many years and failed careers to find his place. His first attempt at work was as a storekeeper's apprentice. But he failed at that because he was too busy talking to sell goods.

Then Henry and his brother—funded by their father—operated their own store. But the brothers weren't cut out for the business. They felt sorry for the poor farmers who had no money. So they extended too much credit and collected too little money. The store went bankrupt in the first year.

Next Henry and his bride, Sallie Shelton, went into tobacco farming. They got off to a good start with 300 acres of land and six slaves provided by Sallie's father. Despite Henry's hard work, he couldn't make a profit from the farm.

Finally Henry found success as a bartender. After the farm failed, Sallie's father invited the family—now including three children—to live in his tavern. Henry proved a very popular host. He often amused guests with his violin. He also had the gift of gab and enjoyed talking politics with customers. Henry always thought over the views he'd heard and then formed his own opinions.

Bartending wasn't enough for Henry. He was ambitious and wanted to be able to support his family.

Henry found the answer to both longings when he met Thomas Jefferson at a party. As a result of their talk, Henry decided to become a lawyer. So he studied for six weeks and set out to get his license. Though he was poorly prepared, the Board of Examination granted the license.

Henry's first important case seemed to be a lost cause. One lawyer had already quit when Henry was called in.

However, Henry proved to be an impressive speaker. Having been poor and unlearned himself, he knew how to speak to ordinary people. He won the case, even though some thought his remarks seemed treasonous.

After this victory, Henry grew to be a popular lawyer. His clever tricks enabled him to free even the guilty.

One time a client of Henry's was charged with pig stealing. The client admitted to Henry that he was guilty. So Henry told the client to cut the dead pig in two. Then he asked for half of the pig as his fee. The man did as ordered.

In court, Henry had his argument ready. He told the judge, "This poor man has no more of that pig than I have. I'll kiss the Bible and take an oath on it."

The man was found innocent.

Henry could win no matter what side of the case he took— even when he took both sides.

One day Henry was called to court to argue a case he wasn't prepared for. In his confusion, he gave a brilliant speech—for the wrong side!

People in the courtroom seemed to be won over by his argument. It looked like a lost cause for Henry's real client.

Henry soon realized his mistake. Without missing a beat he told the court, "I have just stated what I presume is my opponent's side of the case. I shall now show you his reasoning is false, his claims groundless."

continued

With that, Henry made a speech for the opposite side. He won his client's case.

As tension grew in the colonies, so did Henry's interest in politics. He became convinced that America should seek freedom from England. He did his best to convince others of that too. Since he was such a stirring speaker, he won many to his view. He soon became the best-known speaker in America.

Henry was such a popular speaker, he grew a little conceited about his skill. Once Thomas Jefferson was ill and couldn't attend a meeting. So he gave Henry a speech to read.

But Henry didn't think the speech was worth reading. So he threw it away.

Jefferson never forgave him for this, and their once-solid friendship crumbled. From that time on, Henry could do no right in Jefferson's eyes. In fact, until recently, most of what we knew about Henry came from Jefferson's false and vengeful pen.

At the start of the Revolutionary War, Henry was elected commander-in-chief of Virginia's military. But it became clear that Henry's talent did not lie with physical fighting. So he left the army and used his voice as a weapon instead.

In 1776, Henry was elected the first governor of Virginia. He was a popular leader and held that office for five terms.

Though work kept him busy, Henry was very much a family man. He and his wife Sallie had six children. After Sallie's death, Henry married again. He and his second wife had eleven more children.

Henry must have run out of names for all of them. He had two sons named John and two daughters named Martha.

After the war, Henry fought to have a Bill of Rights put into the new U.S. Constitution. He wanted to make sure the new government didn't strip states of their rights. But this time his powerful speaking wasn't enough, and he was outvoted.

Following this defeat, Henry decided he'd had enough of public life. He returned home to spend his time with his family. After all, that must have taken a lot of time. At its largest, Henry's family included 60 grandchildren.

Other than some letters, nothing of what Henry wrote is known to exist. (Jefferson even went so far as to accuse Henry of being totally unable to write.) In fact, the speeches by Henry that we read today are only partly his. Since Henry didn't leave written records of his work, they have been recreated by others.

COMMON SENSE
THOMAS PAINE

VOCABULARY PREVIEW

Below is a list of words that appear in the story. Read the list and get to know the words before you start the story.

abroad—in foreign lands; overseas
advocate—supporter or promoter
civil—of citizens; social
commerce—trade; business
consequences—results or effects
dependent—relying (on) or supported by
distinctions—differences; divisions
enmity—hatred; hostility
extensive—large; wide
fracture—break
imported—from a foreign country; foreign-made
ineffectual—weak or useless
mediators—go-betweens; referees
paradox—puzzle; contradiction
posterity—future generations
prejudice—like or dislike not based on reason; narrow-mindedness
rebels—people who resist their government; rioters or traitors
subjects—citizens
superstition—illogical fear or blind belief
temporary—lasting a short time; not permanent

COMMON SENSE

THOMAS PAINE

The year was 1776. The place was colonial America. And the cause? For Thomas Paine, it was liberty from a bullying government across the ocean. Freedom was waiting for Americans. All that they needed was courage—and a little common sense.

In these pages, I offer nothing more than simple facts, plain arguments, and common sense. I have nothing to settle with the reader beforehand. The only thing that I ask is that he set aside **prejudice** and long-held ideas.

So let him allow his reason and his feelings to decide for themselves. Let him put on—or rather not put off—the true character of man. Then he can widen his views beyond those of today.

Volumes have been written about the struggle between England and America. Men of all ranks have joined the debate. They have done so for different reasons and with different aims. But all have been **ineffectual**. Therefore, the time for debate is over.

As the last resort, arms will decide the contest. This was the choice of the king. And the continent[1] has accepted the challenge.

The late Mr. Pelham was an able prime minister.[2] But he was not without faults. Once he was attacked in the House of Commons[3] because his actions were only of a **temporary** kind. It is reported that he replied, "They will last my time."

Might the colonies[4] hold such deadly or unmanly thoughts in the present contest? If so, the name of ancestors will be remembered in the future with disgust.

The sun never shined on a cause of greater worth. 'Tis[5] not the affair of a city. 'Tis not the affair of a county, a region, or a kingdom. 'Tis the affair of a continent. It concerns an eighth of the globe fit for human life.

'Tis not the concern of a day, a year, or an age. **Posterity** might well be involved in the contest. The future will be more or less affected—even to the end of time—by what happens now.

Now is the time for the seed to be planted of continental union, trust, and honor. The least **fracture** will be very hurtful. As proof, consider this. Suppose that a name was carved with a pin on the bark of a young oak. The wound would enlarge with the tree. Finally posterity would read it in full-grown letters.

By switching from argument to arms, a new era of politics has dawned. A new method of thinking has risen. Plans and

---

[1]Paine means North America.
[2]Henry Pelham was Britain's prime minister from 1744 to 1754.
[3]This is a branch of Parliament, Britain's legislature.
[4]The thirteen colonies were fighting together against England at this time. In the same year *Common Sense* was printed, the Declaration of Independence was signed. The colonies then became the first thirteen states.
[5]An old expression for "it's."

ideas made before April 19—when the fighting began—are like old almanacs.[6] They were proper then. But they have become outdated and useless now.

Back then, people made arguments on either side of the question. But they always arrived at the same point: a union with Great Britain. The only difference between the two sides was how to bring it about. One side suggested force, the other friendship. But it has so far happened that the first has failed. And the second has withdrawn from the argument.

Much has been said about the advantages of reconciliation. These ideas are like a pleasant dream. They have passed away and left us as we were.

It is only right to look at the other side of the question. We should ask what the colonies suffer by being tied to and **dependent** on Great Britain.

We should examine this tie and dependence by the rules of nature and common sense. We should see what we can look forward to if separated. And we should see what we are to expect if we remain dependent.

I have heard this said by some: America has grown strong under her past ties to Great Britain. So the same ties are necessary for her future happiness. These ties will always have the same effect.

Nothing could be more flawed than this kind of argument. We may as well say that a child has lived well on milk. Therefore, it is never to have meat. Or that the first twenty years of our lives should be like the next twenty.

But even this is admitting more than is true. I bluntly answer that America would have grown strong in any case. She probably would have done better had no European power taken any notice of her. The goods of **commerce** which have made America so rich are basic things. She will always have a market while eating is the custom of Europe.

---

[6]An almanac is a yearly calendar with timely facts. Ben Franklin's *Poor Richard's Almanack* is a famous example from the same century.

But Great Britain has protected us, say some. That she has ruled us is true. That she has defended us—at our expense as well as her own—is true. But she would have defended Turkey for the same purpose: trade and power.

Alas![7] We have been long fooled by old prejudices. We have made large sacrifices to **superstition**. We have boasted of the protection of Great Britain.

But we have not considered that her motive was *interest* not *friendship*. She did not protect us from *our enemies on our account*. Instead, she protected us from her enemies on her own account. She protected us from those who had no quarrel with us on any *other account*. These nations will always be our enemies on the *same account*.

Suppose Britain were to give up her claim to the continent. Or suppose the continent were to throw off dependence. We should then be at peace with France and Spain even if they were at war with Britain. The misery of Hanover's last war[8] ought to warn us against such ties.

It has lately been said in Parliament that the colonies are only linked through the parent country. In other words, Pennsylvania, the Jerseys,[9] and the rest are only sister colonies because of England.

This is certainly a very roundabout way of proving relationship. But it is the nearest and only true way of proving **enmity**. (Or enemyship, if I may so call it.)

France and Spain never were our enemies as *Americans*. Perhaps they never will be. Yet they are our enemies as the **subjects** of Great Britain.

But Britain is the parent country, say some. Then the more shame upon her behavior. Even brutes do not devour their young. Even savages do not make war upon their families. So this statement, if true, makes her fault clear.

[7]An expression of sorrow or regret.

[8]"Hanover" is George III, British king during the American Revolution. He came from the Hanover family in Prussia. "Hanover's last war" was the Seven Years War (1756-1763). This began as a conflict between Prussia and Austria. It later affected America and much of Europe. During the war, Britain was Prussia's only major ally.

[9]New Jersey was at one time split into East and West Jersey.

But it happens not to be true—or only partly so. The phrase *parent* or *mother country* has been cleverly used by the king and his followers. It has been used with the low, cunning purpose of prejudicing our weak, trusting minds.

Europe, and not England, is the parent country of America. This new world has been a shelter for the suffering lovers of **civil** and religious liberty. They have come here from *every part* of Europe.

Here have they fled—but not from the tender embraces of the mother. Rather, they have fled from the cruelty of the monster. This is equally true of England. In fact, tyranny—which drove the first Americans from home— still pursues their children.

This is an **extensive** part of the globe. We forget the narrow limits of 360 miles (the length of England). We offer our friendship on a larger scale. We claim brotherhood with every European Christian. We celebrate this generous feeling.

It is pleasant to see how we overcome local prejudices to become friends with the world. The towns in England are divided into parishes.[10] An Englishman will naturally make friends with his parishioners. (This is because their interest in many cases will be common.) He will call him by the name of neighbor.

What if he meets his neighbor but a few miles from home? He drops the narrow idea of street and greets him by the name of townsman.

What if he travels out of the county and meets his neighbor there? He forgets the minor divisions of street and town. He calls him countryman—that is, countyman.

But suppose they should travel in foreign countries? Suppose they should meet in France or any other part of Europe? Then their local identities would be enlarged to that of Englishmen.

---

[10]Like nations, churches divide territory into areas. A parish is a local division made up of one church and one clergyman.

By that same reasoning, all Europeans meeting in America or any other part of the globe are countrymen. For England, Holland, Germany, or Sweden are parts of a whole. On a larger scale, you can compare them to streets, towns, and counties.

Distinctions by nation are too limited for worldly minds. Not one third of our people are of English blood. That is true even of this colony.[11] Therefore, I reject the phrase of *parent* or *mother country* being used for England only. It is false, selfish, narrow, and ungenerous.

But suppose we admit that we are all of English blood. What does it amount to? Nothing. Britain is now an open enemy. This wipes out every other name and title.

And to say that reconciliation is our duty is truly ridiculous. The first king of England—William the Conqueror—was a Frenchman. Half the nobles in England have some French in their blood. By this same reasoning, England ought to be governed by France.

Much has been said of the united strength of Britain and the colonies. It is said that, together, they could defy the world.

But this is just a belief. The outcome of a war is always uncertain. Also, America will never allow itself to be drained of people to support British arms in Asia, Africa, or Europe.

Besides, why should we want to defy the world? Our plan is commerce. If that is well done, it will secure us the peace and friendship of all Europe. After all, it is the interest of all Europe to have America a *free port*. Her trade will always be a protection. And her lack of gold and silver make her safe from invaders.

I challenge the warmest **advocate** for reconciliation to show one advantage to be gained by being tied to Great Britain. I repeat the challenge that not a single advantage can be found. Our corn will fetch a good price in any market in Europe. And our **imported** goods must be paid for, buy them where we will.

---

[11]"This colony" means Pennsylvania.

***

TO CONCLUDE. This may appear strange to some. Or some may be unwilling to think about it. But that does not matter, for many strong and striking reasons all show the same thing. Nothing can settle our problems so quickly as an open and decided DECLARATION FOR INDEPENDENCE.

Some of these reasons are:

First. When two nations are at war, it is often the custom for others to step in. These powers will try to act as **mediators** to bring about peace. But this cannot happen while America calls herself the subject of Great Britain. No country, however well meaning, will offer to mediate. Therefore, in our present state, we may quarrel on forever.

Secondly. It is unreasonable to suppose that France or Spain would assist us. Why should they if we mean only to use their help to repair the break between Britain and America? In this case, France and Spain would only suffer the **consequences** of their aid.

Thirdly. If we keep calling ourselves Britain's subjects, we must be viewed as **rebels** by other nations. This sets a somewhat dangerous example to *their peace.* They fear the idea of those they call subjects taking up arms.

We, on the spot, can solve this **paradox**. But to believe that a rebel can be a subject, too, is a difficult idea for most.

Fourthly. Suppose a declaration were published and sent to foreign governments. In it, we could set forth the miseries we have suffered. It would describe the peaceful methods we have uselessly used to protest.

We also could declare that we can no longer live happily or safely under Britain's cruel rule. It would explain the necessity of breaking off all ties with her.

At the same time, we could assure all nations of our peaceful attitude towards them. We also could express our desire of trading with them. This would bring us more good will than a ship loaded with petitions to Britain.

Being known as British subjects, we cannot be received or heard **abroad**. All countries will be against us. This will be so until we declare independence. Only then will we take our place among other nations.

These actions may seem strange and difficult. But they are like all the other steps which we have already taken. In a little time, they will become familiar and agreeable.

Until independence is declared, the continent will feel like a man who puts off some unpleasant business. He knows it must be done. But he hates to set about it. He wishes it over. Yet he is always haunted by thoughts that it must be done.

INSIGHTS INTO
THOMAS PAINE
(1737-1809)

Paine's early life in England seems like one hard luck story after another. His formal education ended at age 13. At that point his father pulled Paine out of school to teach him staymaking. (Stays were parts of corsets, a woman's undergarment that shaped and narrowed the body.) Then at 17, Paine signed on as a sailor and almost drowned. He tried government work too, but was fired twice. And his own businesses—a corset shop and grocery store—went bankrupt.

Paine's personal relationships were none too happy either. His first wife died in childbirth. His second wife deserted him.

Paine finally decided to seek a new start. So at the age of 37, he set sail for America.

Paine was luckier than most newcomers to America. In the 1770s, many people came as indentured servants. In other words, they swore to serve a master for a set number of years in return for the trip to America. But a settlement payment from his wife gave Paine funds for the voyage.

Paine had something else going for him. He had gotten to know Ben Franklin in England. The two men hit it off. In fact, Franklin wrote Paine a letter of introduction to his son-in-law in America. With such a letter, Franklin's son-in-law would do his best to help Paine.

But when Paine arrived in America, he was too sick to even turn over in bed. Luckily, word leaked out that he

continued

carried letters from Franklin. So some of Franklin's friends carried Paine off the ship and nursed him back to health.

Paine found his place in America as editor of a new journal. Under his leadership, the list of readers swelled. Small wonder, given Paine's talent for taking on big issues in fiery ways.

From his writings, one can see that Paine was often a step ahead of the time. For instance, he wrote articles attacking slavery and pressing for equal rights. He also urged the colonies to separate from Britain. And he was among the first—even before the end of the Revolution—to demand a strong central government.

Some of these articles, especially the ones against slavery, made Paine enemies. But he was never one to care what people thought of him.

When the Revolution started, Paine took the rebels' side. At Franklin's urging, Paine set out to show the conflict from the colonies' view. The result was his pamphlet *Common Sense*. This pamphlet was a huge success in America. Strangely, it sold even more copies in France.

Besides writing pamphlets, Paine also served as secretary to the Committee for Foreign Affairs. Because of this job, Paine learned many important secrets. One such secret was that the American Commissioner to France may not have been totally honest.

Paine decided to write an article detailing his findings. The piece proved to be a firebomb. Congress and many other people grew angry with Paine. They felt these charges may have hurt America's chances of winning the war. The colonies depended on France's aid and couldn't afford to damage that relationship. But as always, Paine was determined to tell the truth.

Because of his "treasonous" writing, Paine grew to be very unpopular. Even friends began to snub him.

One time a stagecoach driver refused to let Paine ride. He feared that God would strike the carriage with lightning. Another report claims a church dismissed its minister for shaking hands with Paine.

After the war the public view of Paine shifted again. The U.S. government realized Paine had greatly helped in the fight for freedom. Congress agreed to give Paine a lump sum of $3,000, plus $800 a year for his efforts. The state of New York also gave him a farm. And Philadelphia awarded Paine $2,500.

Paine's sudden wealth freed him to devote time to science. And he didn't simply study the sciences. He also invented. His projects included the smokeless candle and an engine powered by gunpowder explosions.

Paine's most complex project was the single-arch bridge. Once he finished a model of this bridge, he took it by sled to Franklin's home. Franklin praised the bridge's strength and beauty. He urged Paine to submit it to the French Academy of Science.

However, Paine got nowhere with the French Academy. So he took the design to England. There the bridge was built in a field near London and put on sale. But it seemed no one was interested in buying it.

The bridge was finally put up over England's Weare River. There it stood until 1929. Paine never received a penny for it.

Because of his *Common Sense* pamphlet, Paine was well respected in France. After his bridge was built in England, Paine returned to France to live. In 1792 he became an honorary French citizen.

continued

Paine's honeymoon with France didn't last long. During the French Revolution, he spoke out against the violence. This, plus the fact that he was English by birth, landed Paine in jail for ten months. Only by a lucky accident was his life spared.

When Paine was released from prison, he returned to the U.S. He spent the last years of his life in New York City, living in poverty.

After his death, Paine was buried on his farm in New Rochelle. Even then he was given no peace. His bones were dug up and shipped to England. Today the site of his final grave remains unknown.

Other works by Paine
"African Slavery in America," essay
The Age of Reason, book
The Case of the Officers of Excise, pamphlet
The Crisis, series of pamphlets
The Rights of Man, book

A PLAN FOR MORAL PERFECTION

BENJAMIN FRANKLIN
from Franklin's *AUTOBIOGRAPHY*

VOCABULARY PREVIEW

Below is a list of words that appear in the story. Read the list and get to know the words before you start the story.

chastity—sexual purity; refusal to have sex
constitution—body; health or strength
descendants—children; offspring
frugality—act of saving money; thriftiness
humility—freedom from pride; modesty
inclinations—tendencies; longings
industry—hard work at a job or task; effort
moderation—avoiding of excess or extremes
moral—having to do with right actions
motto—saying; words of wisdom
philosophy—study of truth or knowledge
resolution—firmness (of mind); willpower
sincerity—honesty; openness
successively—one after the other; in order
temperance—self-control, especially in using alcohol; soberness
temptations—forbidden desires
tranquility—peacefulness; calmness
trifling—shallow; unimportant
vices—faults or bad habits
virtuous—decent; upright

A PLAN FOR MORAL PERFECTION

BENJAMIN FRANKLIN

Can humans become perfect? As a young man, Ben Franklin dreamed that it was possible. So he set up a grand scheme to cure himself of all faults. But as Franklin recalls with dry humor in this selection, he wasn't the perfect subject for his perfect scheme.

It was about this time that I came up with a bold and difficult project to reach **moral** perfection.[1] I wished to live without committing any fault at any time. I would conquer all that my natural **inclinations**, habits, or company led me into.

[1] In this section of his autobiography, Franklin writes of his life after 1730.

I knew, or thought I knew, what was right and wrong. So I did not see why I might now *always* do the one and avoid the other.

But I soon found out the task was more difficult than I imagined. While I was carefully guarding against one fault, I was often surprised by another. My habits sometimes took advantage of the fact that I was not paying attention. My inclinations were sometimes too strong for my reason.

I finally decided that it was not enough to believe it was in our best interest to be **virtuous**. That alone would not keep us from slipping. We have to break our bad habits and put good ones in their place. Only then can we be sure of always acting in a virtuous way. For this purpose, I came up with the following method.

I have seen various lists of moral virtues in my reading. I found the lists long or short. It depended on whether the writers included more or fewer ideas under the same name.

Temperance, for example, only applied to eating and drinking according to some. For others, it meant much more. They included all pleasures, appetites, and inclinations. Desires—bodily or mental—were also in their lists. Some even included greed and ambition.

For the sake of clearness, I decided to list more names with fewer ideas under them. That would be better than a few names with more ideas.

I then made a list of thirteen virtues. These were all the ones that struck me as necessary or desirable at the time. Next to each, I wrote a little rule. Those rules fully expressed what I took each virtue to mean.

The virtues and their rules were

1. Temperance. Do not eat to the point where you are overfull. Do not drink to the point of drunkenness.
2. Silence. Speak nothing but what may help others or yourself. Avoid **trifling** conversation.

3. Order. Let all your things have their proper place. Let each part of your business have its proper time.
4. **Resolution.** Resolve to do what you ought. Do without failure whatever you resolve.
5. **Frugality.** Spend nothing except to do good to others and yourself. That is, waste nothing.
6. **Industry.** Lose no time. Always be doing something useful. Cut out all unnecessary actions.
7. **Sincerity.** Do not use hurtful lies. Think innocently and justly. And if you speak, speak innocently and justly as well.
8. Justice. Wrong no one. Do not injure anyone or fail to do good things which are your duty.
9. **Moderation.** Avoid extremes. Do not resent wrongs done to you even though you feel you should.
10. Cleanliness. Allow no uncleanliness in body, clothes, or home.
11. **Tranquility.** Do not be disturbed at trifles or at accidents that are common or cannot be avoided.
12. **Chastity.** Rarely have sex except for health or to have children. Never to the point of becoming weak or dull. Never cause injury to the peace or good name of yourself or another.
13. **Humility.** Imitate Jesus and Socrates.[2]

I intended to make all these virtues a habit. But I judged it would not be good to distract myself by trying all at once.

Instead, I would focus on one of them at a time. When I was the master of one, then I would proceed to another. I would keep doing so till I had gone through all thirteen.

Learning some virtues would make it easier to learn others. Therefore, I arranged them in their above order.

Temperance came first because it tends to make the head

---

[2]Jesus was the founder of Christianity. Socrates (469?-399 B.C.) was a thinker and teacher in ancient Greece.

cool and clear. This is necessary to stay alert and guard against old habits and constant **temptations**.

Once I had mastered that, *silence* would be easier. After all, I desired to gain knowledge as I became virtuous. And in conversation, knowledge is more easily gained by use of the ears than of the tongue.

Therefore, I wanted to break a habit I was getting into of chattering and joking. This habit made me welcome only among trifling people. So I gave silence the second place.

I expected that silence and the next—*order*—would give me more time. This time I could use to spend on my projects and studies.

Resolution, once it became a habit, would keep me firm in my efforts to master all the other virtues.

Frugality and *industry* would free me from my remaining debts. If I were well-off and independent, it would be much easier to practice *sincerity, justice,* etc.

I realized that daily examination would be necessary. This was just the same advice as Pythagoras gave in his golden verses.[3] So I thought up the following method for that examination.

I made a little book. In it, I left a page for each of the virtues. I drew lines on each page with red ink, making seven columns. Thus there was one column for each day of the week. I marked each column with a letter for the day.

I crossed these columns with thirteen red lines. Then I marked the beginning of each line with the first letter of one virtue.

Thus on each line and in its proper column, I could mark a little black spot. This would show my faults for that day.

[3]Pythagoras (582?-500? B.C.) was a Greek thinker and mathematician. His "golden verses" say, "Don't sleep until you have reviewed all your daily activities. Ask yourself three times, 'What have I done wrong? What have I left undone?' "

TEMPERANCE						
Do not eat to the point where you are overfull.						
Do not drink to the point of drunkenness.						

	S	M	T	W	T	F	S
T							
S	••	•		•		•	
O	•	•	•		•	•	•
R			•			•	
F		•			•		
I			•				
S							
J							
M							
Cl.							
T							
Ch.							
H							

I determined to give a week's strict attention to each virtue **successively**. Thus in the first week, I avoided even the least crime against temperance. I left the other virtues to their ordinary chance. I only marked my faults each evening.

Thus my goal was to keep my first line marked "T" clear of spots. If I did that, I could suppose that I had so strengthened my habit in that virtue that I could go to the next. For the following week, I would try to keep both lines clear of spots.

Continuing this way to the last, I could go through a complete course in thirteen weeks. And I could go through four courses in a year.

I would be like a man who has a garden to weed. He does not attempt to get rid of all the weeds at once. That would be beyond his reach and his strength. Instead, he works on one garden bed at a time. Having finished the first, he proceeds to a second.

And so (I hoped) I should have the encouraging pleasure of seeing on my pages the progress I made in virtue. I hoped to successively clear my lines of their spots. In the end, after thirteen weeks, I would be happy to view a clean book.

My little book has as its **motto** these lines from Addison's *Cato*:[4]

Here will I stand. If there is a power above us,
(And there is, as nature proves
Through all her works), he must take delight in virtue.
And whatever he delights in must be blessed.

Another from Cicero:[5]

Oh, **philosophy**, guide of life! You search out virtues and get rid of **vices**! One day lived according to your laws is better than an endless life of sin.

Another from the Proverbs of Solomon speaks of wisdom or virtue:[6]

Long life is in her right hand. In her left hand are riches and fame. Her ways are the ways of pleasantness. All her paths are peaceful.

I believed God to be the fountain of wisdom. Therefore, I thought it right and necessary to ask for his help in obtaining it. For this reason, I made up the following little prayer. I put it in the front of my tables of examination for daily use:

[4]Joseph Addison (1672-1719) was an English playwright. *Cato* was a tragic play he wrote.
[5]Cicero (106-43 B.C.) was an ancient Roman philosopher.
[6]The Proverbs of Solomon are from the Bible.

Oh powerful goodness! Generous father! Merciful guide!
Give me the wisdom to know what are my truest needs.
Strengthen my resolution to do what wisdom says. Accept my kind deeds to your other children. This is all I
can offer in return for your continual favors to me.

I also sometimes used another little prayer. This comes
from Thomson's[7] poems:

Father of light and life, you are the highest good.
O, teach me what is good, teach me what you are!
Save me from folly, vanity, vice,
and every foul activity. Fill my soul
with knowledge, peace, and pure virtue.
Bring me sacred, real, and never-fading bliss!

I remembered my rule of *order*. This required that *every
part of my business should have its proper time*. So one page
in my little book contained the following scheme for using
the twenty-four hours of the day:

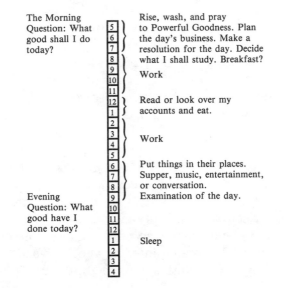

The Morning Question: What good shall I do today?	5 6 7 8	Rise, wash, and pray to Powerful Goodness. Plan the day's business. Make a resolution for the day. Decide what I shall study. Breakfast?
	9 10 11	Work
	12 1	Read or look over my accounts and eat.
	2 3 4 5	Work
Evening Question: What good have I done today?	6 7 8 9	Put things in their places. Supper, music, entertainment, or conversation. Examination of the day.
	10 11 12 1 2 3 4	Sleep

[7]James Thomson (1700-1748) was an English poet. These lines are from the
"Winter" section of *The Seasons*.

I started carrying out this plan of self-examination. And I continued it with occasional breaks for some time. I was surprised to find myself much fuller of faults than I had imagined. But I had the satisfaction of seeing them grow fewer.

I erased the marks of old faults to reuse my tables. Therefore, my little book became full of holes.

So here is how I avoided the trouble of restoring my little book now and then. I copied my charts and lines to the smoother pages of a memo book. Its lines were drawn with long-lasting red ink. On these lines, I marked my faults with a black lead pencil. I could easily wipe these out with a wet sponge.

After a while, I went through only one course in a year. Afterwards, I went through only one in several years. At length, I stopped them entirely. I was too busy with voyages, business, and many other things. But I always carried my little book with me.

My rule of *order* gave me the most trouble. I found that it might have worked where a man's business gave him control over his time. A printer might be an example.

But it cannot be exactly followed by a man in charge of others. He must mix with the world. Often he has to receive business people when they are free.

Order was also difficult for me to learn with regard to places for things, papers, and so forth. I hadn't learned it while young. Besides, I had a very good memory. So I was not as aware of the problems coming from poor planning.

Therefore, this rule cost me a great deal of painful concern. My faults in it bothered me. And I made very little progress in mending them. Moreover, I had frequent relapses. I was almost ready to give up the attempt and content myself with a faulty character.

I was like the man who bought an ax from my neighbor, the smith.[8] The man wanted its whole surface to be as bright as its edge. The smith agreed to grind it bright for him. But

[8]Or *blacksmith*, one who works with iron.

he asked the man to turn the wheel.

So the man turned. Meanwhile, the smith pressed the broad face of the ax hard and heavily on the stone wheel. This made the turning of it very tiring.

Now and then, the man would leave the wheel to see how the work was going. At length he was ready to take the ax as it was without further grinding.

"No," said the smith. "Turn on, turn on. We shall have it bright by and by. As yet, 'tis⁹ only speckled."

"Yes," said the man. "But *I think I like a speckled ax best.*"

And I believe this may have been the case with many others who lacked a method like mine. They have discovered how hard it was to learn good habits and break bad ones. They have given up the struggle and concluded that *a speckled ax was best.*

And something that pretended to be reason spoke to me now and then. It suggested that the perfection I demanded of myself might be a kind of showiness in morals. If what I expected of myself became known, it would make me look ridiculous.

Besides, a perfect character might go along with the problem of being envied or hated. A kindly man should allow a few faults in himself to keep his friends happy.

In truth, I found myself impossible when it came to *order*. Now that I have grown old and my memory bad, I feel the lack of it very strongly.

So I never reached the perfection I had been so eager to obtain. In fact, I fell far short of it. But on the whole, I became a better and happier man by the effort than I would otherwise have been.

I was like those who aim at perfect writing by imitating models out of a book. They may never reach the wished-for excellence of those models. But their handwriting is improved by the effort. And it is acceptable as long as it is nice and readable.

⁹An old-fashioned way of saying "it's."

And it may be well to say that posterity should be informed of this: Their ancestor owed the constant happiness of his life to this practice and the blessing of God. This had been true down to his seventy-ninth year, in which this is written.

What troubles may come during the remainder of his life is in the hands of God. But if they arrive, memories of past happiness ought to help him bear them with more patience.

To *temperance* he owes his long-continued health and what is still left of his good **constitution**.

To *industry* and *frugality* he owes the early easiness of his life. They made it possible for him to gain the fortune and knowledge which allowed him to be a useful citizen. And through them he gained some measure of fame among the learned.

To *sincerity* and *justice* he owes the trust and honorable duties his country granted to him.

And to the combined influence of the whole mass of virtues, he owes much. Even in an imperfect state, he was able to acquire them. He owes to them all his evenness of temper and his cheerfulness in conversation. This makes his company still sought for and pleasant, even to his younger friends.

I hope, therefore, that some of my **descendants** may follow this example and benefit.

INSIGHTS INTO
BENJAMIN FRANKLIN
(1706-1790)

Ben Franklin had only two years of schooling. However, he became one of the best-educated men of his time. That's because he read every book he could get his hands on. In the course of his study, he taught himself algebra, geometry, navigation, grammar, logic, and science.

At age 12, Franklin started his printing career as an apprentice to his brother, James. Young Ben felt inspired to write for his brother's paper. However, James refused to publish any of Ben's work.

Ben wrote the articles anyway. Then after signing them "Mrs. Silence Dogood," he slipped them under the print-shop door.

The articles impressed James and he printed several. But when he found out who the real author was, he refused to publish any more. Then James realized how popular the Dogood articles were. So he unwillingly agreed to keep printing them.

The problems between the brothers continued. Finally, at the age of 17, Franklin escaped by running away to Philadelphia.

Yet the rocky years with James didn't affect Franklin's love for his job. Despite all his later deeds, he began his will with these words: "I, Benjamin Franklin, printer . . . "

continued

Once in Philadelphia, Franklin and a friend set up a print shop. But soon the friend left, so Franklin operated it on his own.

Franklin didn't lack for company in his shop. His wife often helped him. And his three children spent much time playing there.

Franklin enjoyed his printing work. But he missed the newspaper business too. So he bought several newspapers to publish. Not all of these papers made money. Yet Franklin published them anyway as a public service.

For Franklin, serving the public didn't stop with newspapers. He also became Philadelphia's postmaster. In this role he organized city-wide mail service and the first dead-letter office. (This job gave Franklin a bonus. It allowed him to receive news for his papers more quickly.)

In addition, Franklin started the world's first subscription library. Members gave money to buy books and then borrowed them for free. He also set up the city's first fire department and started a program of road paving. Plus he helped found a hospital as well as a school (which became the University of Pennsylvania).

Franklin held mostly low-level public offices. (For example, for nineteen years, he was elected clerk of the state assembly.) Yet he proved one of the most influential men in America. He was the only person who signed all four of these important American documents: the Declaration of Independence, the Treaty of Alliance with France, the Treaty of Peace with Great Britain, and the Constitution.

Franklin was famous not only in America. He was well respected in Europe too, where he served as a diplomat. He was able to convince France to become an ally of the American colonies. Without France's help, the Revolutionary War might have ended in an American defeat.

With such a busy life, it's a wonder Franklin found time to enjoy his favorite hobby: science. Yet he did. He was one of the first to experiment with electricity. His famous kite flight proved that lightning was a form of electricity. As a result of this experiment, Franklin invented the lightning rod.

Franklin's endless curiosity led him to many other discoveries. Among his inventions are the electric battery, the Franklin stove, and bifocal eyeglasses. He also created the harmonica.

But Franklin refused to patent (protect from copying) his inventions or sell them for profit. He only wanted to figure things out and make life more convenient for others.

Even after his death, Franklin helped his country. In his will he left money to Boston and Philadelphia. Franklin asked that the sums be used to aid "young men of good character" in following a trade or craft.

Franklin's wishes were obeyed. The interest on his money has been used to support schools, students, museums, and loans to workers.

Franklin directed that two hundred years after his death, all the money (not just the interest) be used by the cities. In Philadelphia, that sum came to $520,000. In Boston, it amounted to $4.5 million. Both cities decided to stick to Franklin's intent by using the money to help train people in trades and crafts.

Other works by Franklin
  The Dogood Papers, book
  Poor Richard Improved, book
  Poor Richard's Almanack, book
  "Rules by Which a Great Empire May Be Reduced to
    a Small One," essay
  The Way to Wealth, book

SELF-RELIANCE
RALPH WALDO EMERSON

VOCABULARY PREVIEW

Below is a list of words that appear in the story. Read the list and get to know the words before you start the story.

bigot—a person who dislikes those of other races, religions, etc.

committed—bound; obliged

conforms—obeys; consents

consistency—sameness, regularity, or order

conventional—usual; traditional

corpse—dead body

disdain—scorn; hate

enviable—pleasing; desirable

eternal—the everlasting or undying; (also, in the context of this essay, God)

genius—great natural talent or ability; brilliance

hobgoblin—consideration or concern (especially something that causes unnecessary concern)

integrity—honesty; sincerity

muse—inspiration; creative spark

penances—acts done to show sorrow for sins or crimes

philanthropy—love of humankind; charity

solitude—aloneness; privacy

spectacle—public display; exhibit

transcendent—magnificent; extraordinary

unbiased—fair; open-minded

whim—sudden desire or notion

SELF-RELIANCE

RALPH WALDO EMERSON

"Trust Yourself."

**That seems simple enough advice.
Yet as Emerson warns in this essay,
it's probably the toughest
but most important rule
you'll ever learn.**

Do not search outside yourself.
—Persius[1]

Man is his own star. A man with a soul which makes
Him honest and perfect
Will command all light, all power, all fate.
Nothing will come to that man too early or late.
Our acts are our angels, for good or ill.
They are our shadows, following us always.
—Beaumont and Fletcher[2]

[1]Persius (34-62) was an ancient Roman poet. His words mean that a person
shouldn't imitate others but rely on himself or herself.
[2]Beaumont and Fletcher were English playwrights who lived at the same time as
Shakespeare. They wrote a great number of plays together.

Throw the babe on the rocks.
Nurse him with the she-wolf's milk.
If he winters with the hawk and fox,
Power and speed will be his hands and feet.
                                    —Emerson

The other day I read some verses by a well-known painter. They were original and not **conventional**. The soul always hears advice in such lines, whatever the subject is. The sentiments they awaken are of more value than any thought they may contain.

What, then, is **genius?** It is to believe in your own thought. It is to believe that what is true for you in your private heart is true for all men.

Speak your secret beliefs and you shall find they are true for everyone. For always what is inner shall become outer. And the trumpets of the Last Judgment[3] will echo back to us our first thoughts.

The voice of the mind is familiar to each person. Yet we praise Moses, Plato, and Milton[4] most highly because they did not value books and traditions. They spoke not what others thought but what they thought.

A man should learn to detect and watch that gleam of light which flashes within the mind. He should pay more attention to it than to the heavenly visions of poets and wise men. Yet he often dismisses his thought just because it is his own.

In every work of genius, we recognize our own rejected thoughts. They come back to us with a certain familiar greatness.

Great works of art have no more powerful lesson for us than this. They teach us to stand by our first impressions

---

[3]In Christian belief, the Last Judgment is the day God decides the final fate of every human.

[4]In the Bible, Moses was a Hebrew leader who gave his people the Ten Commandments. Plato (427?-347 B.C.) was a Greek philosopher. Milton (1608-1674) was a famous English poet.

with cheerful firmness. They teach us to do so even when everyone is against us.

Otherwise, tomorrow some stranger will say exactly and with great good sense what we thought and felt all along. And so we shall have to shamefully learn our own opinion from another.

There is a time when every man arrives at the belief that envy is ignorance and imitation is suicide. He sees that he must take himself as he is, for better or worse.

He realizes, too, that the wide universe is full of good. Even so, he will have no nourishing corn unless he farms the ground that has been given to him.

The power in every single man is a new thing in nature. He doesn't know what he can do until he has tried.

There is a reason one face, one person, one fact impresses him and another does not. This sculpture in the memory is evidence of a planned harmony. The eye was placed where one ray should fall so it might tell about that ray.

Let each man bravely and fully tell the world what he sees and knows. We only half express ourselves. We seem ashamed of the divine idea within us.

Something is accepted as reasonable and helpful if it is done from the heart. But God will not have his work made public by cowards. It takes a divine man to do anything divine.

A man is relieved and happy when he has put his heart into his work and done his best. But he will have no peace when he has said or done otherwise. It is a deliverance which does not deliver. When a man does things half-heartedly, his genius deserts him. No **muse** befriends him. No fresh ideas or hope arises.

Trust yourself. Every heart echoes to that firm rule. Accept the place that God has found for you. Accept the society of your fellow man and the connection of events.

Great men have always done so. They have entrusted themselves like children to the spirit of their age. They have revealed their belief that the **Eternal** was stirring in their hearts. They knew it was working through their hands, ruling their whole being.

We are now men and must accept the same **transcendent** destiny. We must not be pinched into a corner. We must not act like cowards fleeing before a revolution.

Instead, we must become rescuers and helpers. We must become holy and noble clay for the Almighty to mold. Let us march upon confusion and darkness.

What pretty support for this lesson we can find in nature. We see it in the faces and behavior of babies, children, and even animals. Unlike them, our minds are often divided. We do not trust our feelings because we have computed that the odds are against us.

But children do not do this. Their minds are whole. Their eye is still fresh. So when we look into their faces, we are disturbed.

An infant **conforms** to nobody. Everyone conforms to it. One babe often turns four or five adults into babies, too. For proof, see how they coo and play with it.

In the same way, God has given youths, teenagers, and adults their own appeal and charm. He has made each **enviable** and pleasant. Each has charms that cannot be denied.

Do not think the youth has no force because he cannot speak to you and me. Listen! In the next room, who spoke so clear and forcefully?

Good Heaven! It is he! It is that very lump of shyness and laziness who has done nothing for weeks except eat! And now he rolls out these words like a ringing bell. It seems he knows how to speak to those of his own age. So, shy or bold, he will know how to make us adults unnecessary before long.

Watch how easygoing boys are who are sure of their dinner. Like a lord, they would **disdain** to do or say anything just to keep the peace. This is the healthy attitude of human nature.

Such a boy is the master of society. He is both independent and reckless. He looks out from his corner at people and facts as they pass by. He judges and sentences them by their merits in the swift, direct way of boys. He calls them good, bad, interesting, silly, moving, or troublesome.

He never bothers himself about consequences or what others want. Instead, he gives an independent, truthful decision. You must persuade him. He does not try to persuade you.

Once the youth is a man, it is as though he has been jailed by his very thoughts. As soon as he acts or speaks just once with glory, then he is **committed**. Hundreds are watching him, either in sympathy or hatred. Now he must take their feelings into account. There is no Lethe for this.[5]

Ah, that a man could go back to his free, godlike independence! The man who can take back all promises will always be strong. One who always sees things with the same **unbiased**, unfrightened innocence will always earn the respect of poets and others.

One like this, who is always young, would make his power felt. He would utter opinions about all events. These views would not seem merely private but important to everyone. They would sink like darts into the ears of other men and put them in fear.

These are the voices which we hear when we are alone. They grow faint and hard to hear whenever we enter into the world.

Society everywhere tries to scheme against the manhood of every one of its members. It is like a joint-stock company.[6] In order for the shareholders to get bread, the members agree to give up liberty and ideas.

Most of the time, the most valued virtue is conformity. Self-reliance is its opposite. Conformity does not love realities and creators. Instead, it loves names and customs.

Whoever wants to be a man must be a nonconformist. He who would gather lasting fame must not be held back

---

[5]In Greek myths, Lethe is a river in the Underworld. Drinking from it made a person forget everything.

[6]A joint-stock company is one where the wealth of the company is divided into shares owned by shareholders.

by what people call goodness. Instead, he must explore what goodness really is.

In the end, nothing is sacred but the **integrity** of our own mind. Approve of yourself and you shall have the approval of the world.

I remember something I once said to a valued adviser when I was quite young. This man often badgered me with the dear old beliefs of the church.

I would say to him, "Why should I worry about the holiness of traditions? I live wholly from within."

"But your impulses may come from below, not from above," suggested my friend.[7]

I replied, "They don't seem to me to be from below. But if I am to be the devil's child, I will live from the devil."

No law can be sacred to me except a law from myself. Good and bad are just names very easily transferred to that or this. The only right is what suits my nature. The only wrong is what is against it.

A man should act in the face of all opposition as if everything were empty and short-lived except himself. I am ashamed to think how easily we surrender to badges and names. How easily we give in to large societies and dead customs.

Every decent, well-spoken person affects and sways more than is right. I ought to act honestly and forcefully, speaking the rude truth in all ways.

If hatred and selfishness wear the coat of **philanthropy**, shall I let that pass?

Suppose an angry **bigot** takes up the cause of Abolition?[8] Suppose he comes to me telling the latest news from Barbados?[9] Why should I not say to him:

"Go love thy[10] babe. Love thy woodchopper. Be good-natured and modest. Learn these virtues. And never try to

---

[7]That is, they may come from the devil and not from God.
[8]Abolitionism was a movement in the 19th century to outlaw slavery.
[9]Barbados is an island in the West Indies. Slavery was outlawed there in 1834, and all slaves were freed by 1838.
[10]"Thy" is an old-fashioned word for "your."

cover your hard, selfish ambition with this false tenderness for black folk a thousand miles off. Thy love for those far away is really hatred at home.''

This greeting would be rough and graceless. But truth is handsomer than pretended love. Your goodness must have an edge to it—or else it is not goodness. Hatred must be preached to combat love when it whimpers and whines.

I avoid father and mother and wife and brother when my genius calls me.[11] I want to write on my doorpost: **Whim.**[12] I hope it proves to be somewhat better than a whim in the end. But we cannot spend all day explaining. Do not expect me to tell why I seek or why I avoid company.

Then, again, do not tell me—as a good man did today—of my duty to help the poor. Are they *my* poor?

I tell you this, foolish philanthropist. I grudge every dollar, dime, and cent I give to those who do not belong to me and to whom I do not belong.

There is a class of persons to whom I am deeply spiritually drawn. For them, I will go to prison if need be.

But there are various other popular charities. Funds for the education of fools at college. The building of meeting halls for that useless purpose that many now fill. Money to drunks. The thousands of Relief Societies.

I shamefully confess that I sometimes give a dollar to such causes. Yet it is a wicked dollar. By and by, I shall have the courage to withhold it.

Virtues are commonly thought of as the exception rather than the rule. We speak of a man *and* his virtues. Men do what is called a good action—a deed of courage or charity— much as they would pay a fine for doing wrong. Their deeds are done as an apology or an excuse for living. Like the sickly and insane, they pay dearly for their care. Their virtues are

---

[11]The book of Matthew in the Bible directs a person to avoid family in order to obey a command from God.

[12]In the Bible, God orders Moses to mark with blood the doors of every Jew's house. This sign protects the Jews when God kills ''all the firstborn in the land of Egypt, both man and beast.'' Emerson wants a similar protection. By writing ''whim'' on his door, he hopes to keep out visitors.

but **penances**.

I do not wish to do penance but to live. My life is not an apology but a life. It is for itself and not a **spectacle**.

I do not want a glittering and unsteady life. I would prefer it to be less spectacular, so long as it is genuine and balanced. I wish it to be healthy and sweet, not to need careful diet and bleeding.[13] My life should be unique. It should be a charity, a battle, a conquest, a medicine.

I ask for firsthand evidence that you are a man. Refuse to do things for the sake of their supposed goodness. As for myself, it makes no difference if I do or do not do those things which are judged excellent. But I cannot consent to pay for a privilege which is mine by rights.

My talents may be few and unworthy. But I actually exist. I need no further proof for my own sake or that of my fellows.

What I must do is all that concerns me. What people think does not matter. This is an equally hard rule in actual and intellectual life. Yet it makes the whole difference between greatness and smallness.

The rule is all the harder because you always find those who think they know your duty better than you do. In public, it is easy to fit in with public opinion. In **solitude**, it is easy to live according to your own views. But the great man is he who, with perfect sweetness, remains independent in public.

I object to conforming to dead customs because it scatters your force. It wastes your time and blurs the impression you can make.

You may support a dead church or give to a dead Bible Society. You may vote along with a great party either for the government or against it. You may set your table like any lowly housekeeper.

Behind all these screens, I have difficulty telling exactly

---

[13]Bleeding is an old medical treatment once thought to help cure a person of disease or weakness.

who you are. And, of course, those screens take away force from your proper life. But do your thing, and I shall know you. Do your work, and you shall strengthen yourself.

A man must consider what a blindman's bluff[14] this game of conformity is. If I know your religion, I can anticipate your argument.

I hear a preacher announce his sermon to be the correctness of a church belief. Do I not already know he cannot possibly say anything new? Do I not know that despite his promises to examine the belief, he will do no such thing? Do I not know that he has pledged to look at only one side? The permitted side?

And he will look not as a man but as a minister. He is just a hired attorney. His lawyer-like manners are the emptiest kind of show.

Well, most men are blindfolded with one handkerchief or another. They have joined some group and accepted its opinion. This conformity makes them false in not just a few ways but in all ways. A teller of not just a few lies but many.

Every truth they tell is not quite true. Their two is not the real two. Their four not the real four. Every word they say troubles us. We do not know how to set them right.

Meantime, nature is not slow to fit us with the prison uniform of the party to which we belong. We come to wear one type of face and figure. Little by little, we take on a gentle, foolish expression.

There is one shameful experience in particular which this leads to. I am speaking of "the foolish face of praise."[15] This is the false smile we wear when we feel uneasy in talking about that which does not interest us.

This smile does not come naturally but is forced. The muscles grow tight around the outline of the face and create an unpleasant feeling. It is a feeling of being scolded and warned. No brave young man will suffer it twice.

---

[14]This is a game in which a blindfolded person tries to catch another player and guess who that person is.
[15]Emerson is quoting the English poet Alexander Pope (1688-1744).

When you do not conform, the world whips you with its displeasure. . . . You need a big heart and religion to treat the anger of the people as something of no concern.

The other terror that scares us from self-trust is our **consistency**. We respect too much our past act or word because others have only that basis for predicting what we will do. So we are reluctant to disappoint them.

But why should you keep looking over your shoulder? Why drag around this monstrous **corpse** of your memory for fear you should contradict what you have said? Suppose you should contradict yourself? What then?

It seems to be a rule of wisdom never to rely on your memory alone. This rule holds true even in acts of pure memory. It seems wiser to judge the past in terms of the thousand-eyed present and always live in the present.

Trust your emotion. In your study of religion, you have denied human qualities in God. Yet when religious feelings touch your soul, offer them heart and life. Do so even if that means giving God a shape and personality. Leave your earlier notions behind. Leave them as Joseph left his coat in the hand of the harlot, and flee.[16]

A foolish consistency is the **hobgoblin** of little minds. It is adored by little politicians, philosophers, and preachers. A great soul has simply nothing to do with consistency. He may as well concern himself with his shadow on the wall.

Enough of your guarded lips! Sew them with thread. If you would be a man, speak what you think today in words as hard as cannonballs. Then speak what you think tomorrow in hard words again. Do this even though it contradicts everything you said today.

"Ah, but then you are sure to be misunderstood!" exclaim the old ladies.

Misunderstood! It is a word for perfect fools! Is it so bad, then, to be misunderstood!

---

[16]A harlot, in this case, is a woman of low moral character. The Bible tells how Joseph was tempted by another man's wife. He tried to ignore her, but one day she grabbed him by his coat and wouldn't let go. Joseph slipped out of his coat and ran.

Pythagoras was misunderstood. So were Socrates, and Jesus, and Luther. Copernicus, Galileo, and Newton were misunderstood, too.[17]

So was every pure and wise spirit that ever lived. To be great is to be misunderstood.

[17]Pythagoras was an ancient Greek philosopher. So was Socrates. Jesus was the founder of Christianity, and Martin Luther founded Protestantism. Copernicus was an astronomer. Galileo and Newton were great physicists.

INSIGHTS INTO
RALPH WALDO EMERSON
(1803-1882)

Ralph Waldo Emerson began his career of learning at an early age. He started school when he was two. By age three, he was able to read.

Emerson enjoyed his classes for the most part. But he also liked to skip school sometimes. On these heavenly days, he played in the fields and woods.

Yet in a sense, Emerson was still at school even outdoors. Nature fascinated him. He studied wildlife as closely as he did his books.

Emerson did manage to steal some hours for play. But more often, his free time was spent doing household chores.

By the time he was eight, Emerson faced more adult duties. That year his minister father died.

Mr. Emerson's church helped support Mrs. Emerson and her eight children. But the young family still struggled.

One year money was especially hard to come by. That winter, young Ralph had to share a coat with one of his brothers. The pain of the cold was bad enough. What the brothers hated just as much was being laughed at by schoolmates.

At age seventeen, Emerson entered Harvard University. To help pay for his studies, he worked as an errand boy for the school's president.

Emerson graduated in 1821 with a so-so school record. He had barely managed to stay in the top half of his class.

And even being named class poet wasn't much of an honor. He took the title only after seven other students had turned it down.

After college, Emerson became a teacher for a short while. This job didn't suit him, so he entered the Harvard Divinity School. The choice seemed a natural one. Many of Emerson's relatives had been ministers.

Yet Emerson never felt a real urge to be a minister. So it isn't surprising that he left the pulpit after just three years.

Emerson's decision to leave didn't mean that he stopped believing in God. But he saw God in everyday people, things, and actions more than in church. This view became the focus of many of his poems and essays.

Emerson and his second wife, Lidian, had four children. Emerson dearly loved his family, especially his son Waldo.

Emerson was not fated to enjoy Waldo for long. The boy died of scarlet fever when he was five.

This loss was the fourth Emerson had recently suffered. His first wife and two of his brothers had died all within a few years. So Waldo's death was even harder to bear. Emerson's moving poem "Threnody," written in honor of Waldo, captures his pain.

Emerson found other comforts besides writing verses. As he had done from his boyhood, he took to walking through the woods. Once he and his friend Nathaniel Hawthorne covered twenty miles in a single day!

Hawthorne wasn't the only famous author Emerson could claim as a friend. Others were Oliver Wendell Holmes and Henry Wadsworth Longfellow. He was also teacher and friend to Louisa May Alcott, author of *Little Women*.

continued

Henry David Thoreau was another friend. He actually lived with the Emersons for a while as handyman.

Emerson made his living by speaking as well as writing. And his voice proved as powerful in the lecture hall as on paper. People in both America and Europe flocked to hear him speak.

Though a great speaker, Emerson was viewed by his friends as cool and withdrawn. But with his family, he was warm and fun-loving. Even so, he didn't believe in laughing out loud, even at the funniest joke.

Emerson and his family lived in a big house near Walden Pond in Concord. When Emerson wasn't on the road lecturing, he was at home writing.

Another of Emerson's at-home loves was gardening. However, he was very clumsy with a spade. His son once saw him at work in the yard. Alarmed, he yelled, "Look out, Papa, you'll dig your leg!"

In 1872, these peaceful days at Walden Pond ended. That year the Emersons' home caught fire. Neighbors rushed to help. But much of the house was destroyed.

Soon after, friends raised money and sent Emerson and his daughter to Europe. When the two returned, they received a great surprise. The townspeople respected Emerson so much, they had rebuilt his house for him.

The shock of the fire caused Emerson to grow very ill. Sadly, his mind was the first to go. Simple words began to escape him. For example, instead of saying "chair," he said "that which supports the human frame."

Emerson still knew faces. But he often forgot the names that went with them. This failing was obvious at the funeral of his friend Longfellow. Twice Emerson went to the coffin and stared at the dead man's face. Then he remarked,

"That gentleman was a sweet, beautiful soul. But I have completely forgotten his name."

Soon after this, Emerson caught pneumonia. He never recovered. He died in 1882, one of the most respected American writers of his time.

Other works by Emerson
"The American Scholar," lecture
The Conduct of Life, book
Essays, First Series, book
Essays, Second Series, book
Nature, book
"The Rhodora," poem
"Terminus," poem

CLIMBING FROM THE TOMB OF SLAVERY

FREDERICK DOUGLASS
from *NARRATIVE OF THE LIFE OF FREDERICK DOUGLASS*

VOCABULARY PREVIEW

Below is a list of words that appear in the story. Read the list and get to know the words before you start the story.

adultery—sex between a married person and someone other than his/her mate; unfaithfulness in marriage
compensation—payment; reward
comply—obey; give in
defiance—challenge or rebellion
dense—closely packed; thick
disposition—nature or character; also, tendency or inclination
dregs—worst part (literally, the bits of solid material that sink to the bottom of a liquid)
endurance—hardship; suffering
forte—strong point; specialty
justify—show cause for; make excuses for
lingering—remaining; staying
matted—tangled
multitude—mass; group
resistance—opposition; refusal
resurrection—rebirth; new life
revived—awakened; renewed
shrouded—veiled; hidden
stupor—dreamlike state; daze
unaccountable—unexplainable; odd
yoked—joined together with a yoke (crossbar)

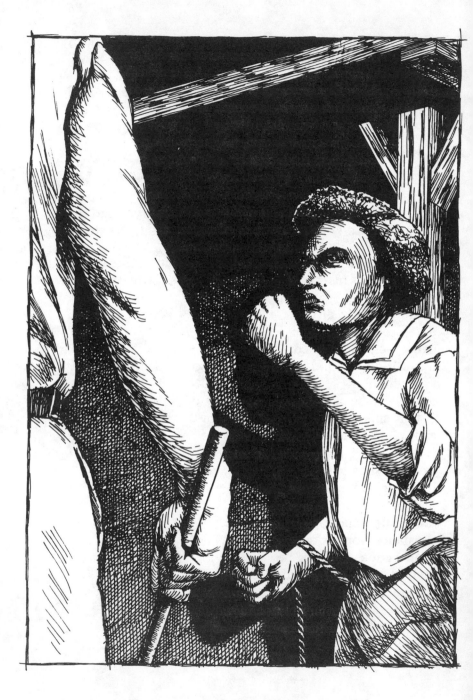

CLIMBING from the TOMB of SLAVERY

FREDERICK DOUGLASS

What picture comes to mind when you hear the word "slave"?
A person in chains, head bowed and hope gone? Perhaps true in
some cases, but not for Frederick Douglass. In this selection, the one-
time slave proves that no chain is strong enough to bind the human spirit.

I left Master Thomas's house and went to
live with Mr. Covey on January 1, 1833.[1] I was
now, for the first time in my life, a field hand.
In my new job, I found myself awkward. I was
even more awkward than seems a country boy
in a large city.

[1] At the time of the story, Douglass was 16 years old and a slave. His owner, Master
Thomas Auld, had rented him out to Mr. Covey. Auld was a cruel master.
Determined to crush Douglass' spirit, Auld turned him over to a professional
"Negro-breaker."

I had been at my new home but one week when Mr. Covey gave me a very severe whipping. He cut my back, causing the blood to run. And he raised ridges on my flesh as large as my little finger.

The details of this affair are as follows. Mr. Covey sent me very early one morning to get a load of wood. It was one of the coldest days in the month of January.

Mr. Covey gave me a team of unbroken oxen.[2] He told me which was the in-hand ox and which the off-hand one. He tied the end of the rope around the horns of the in-hand ox. Then he gave me the other end of it. He told me that if the oxen started to run, I must hold onto the rope.

I had never driven oxen before. So, of course, I was very awkward. However, I succeeded in getting to the edge of the woods with little difficulty. But after I had gotten a few rods[3] into the woods, the oxen took fright. They started going full speed. They carried the cart against trees and over stumps in the most frightful manner. I expected every moment that my brains would be dashed out against the trees.

They ran thus for a great distance. At last, they finally upset the cart. They dashed it with great force against a tree and threw themselves into a **dense** thicket. How I escaped death, I do not know.

There I was, entirely alone. I was in a thick wood in a place new to me. My cart was upset and shattered. My oxen were tangled up among the young trees. And there was no one to help me.

After a long effort, I succeeded in getting my cart upright and my oxen untangled. Then I again **yoked** them to the cart.

I now proceeded on with my team to the place where I had, the day before, been chopping wood. There I loaded my cart pretty heavily. I thought that in this way, I could tame my oxen.

Then I proceeded on my way home. I had now wasted

[2]Oxen are animals related to cattle and buffalo. "Unbroken" means untamed. In a team of oxen, the "in-hand" ox is on the left and the "off-hand" ox is on the right.
[3]A rod is a unit of measure equal to 5½ yards.

one half of the day.

I got out of the woods safely and now felt out of danger. I stopped my oxen to open the gate.

Just as I did so, the oxen again started. I had no time to get hold of my ox rope, so they rushed through the gate.

Catching the gate between the wheel and the body of the cart, they tore it to pieces. And they came within a few inches of crushing me against the gate post. Thus twice, in one short day, I escaped death by slightest chance.

On my return, I told Mr. Covey what had happened and how. He ordered me to return to the woods immediately. I did so, and he followed on after me.

Just as I got into the woods, he came up and told me to stop my cart. He said he would teach me how to trifle away my time and break gates.

He then went to a large gum tree. With his axe, he cut three large switches.[4] After trimming them neatly with his pocketknife, he ordered me to take off my clothes.

I made him no answer but stood with my clothes on. He repeated his order. I still made him no answer. Nor did I move to strip myself.

Upon this he rushed at me with the fierceness of a tiger. He tore off my clothes and lashed me till he had worn out his switches. He cut me so savagely that he left marks that could be seen for a long time after.

This whipping was the first of a number just like it and for similar mistakes.

I lived with Mr. Covey one year. During the first six months of that year, scarcely a week passed without his whipping me. I was seldom free from a sore back. My awkwardness was almost always his excuse for whipping me.

We were worked fully up to the point of **endurance**. Long before day we were up and our horses fed. By the first approach of day, we were off to the field with our hoes and plowing teams.

Mr. Covey gave us enough to eat but scarce time to eat

[4]A switch is a bendable stick used as a whip.

it. We were often allowed less than five minutes to take our meals.

We were often in the field from daybreak till the sun's last **lingering** ray had left us. We were there even longer at haying time. Midnight often caught us in the field binding hay.

Covey would be out with us. The way he used to stand it was this. He would spend the most of his afternoons in bed and come out fresh in the evening. He was then ready to urge us on with words, example, and often whip.

Mr. Covey was one of the few slaveholders who could and did work with his hands. He was a hard-working man. He knew by himself just what a man or boy could do. There was no deceiving him.

His work went on in his absence almost as well as in his presence. He had the ability to make us feel that he was ever present with us. This he did by surprising us.

He seldom approached the spot where we were at work openly. If he could, he would do it secretly. He always aimed at taking us by surprise. He was so cunning that, among ourselves, we used to call him "the snake."

Sometimes when we were at work in the cornfield, he would crawl on his hands and knees to avoid being seen. Then, all at once, he would rise in our midst. He would scream out, "Ha, ha! Come, come! Dash on, dash on!"

As this was his means of attack, it was never safe to stop a single minute. His comings were like a thief in the night. He appeared to us to be always at hand. He was under every tree on the plantation and behind every stump. He was in every bush and at every window.

He would sometimes mount his horse as if going to St. Michael's,[5] a distance of seven miles. But half an hour afterwards, you would see him. He would be coiled in the corner of the wood fence, watching every motion of the slaves. He would, for this purpose, leave his horse tied up in the woods.

[5]St. Michael's is a town in Maryland. Maryland was the northernmost of the slave states.

At other times, he would walk up to us and give us orders as though he were about to start on a long journey. Then he would turn his back and seem as though he were going to the house to get ready.

But he would stop short before he would get halfway there. He would turn and crawl into a fence corner or behind some tree. There he would watch us till the going down of the sun.

Mr. Covey's **forte** was his power to deceive. His life was devoted to planning and carrying out the greatest deceptions. He made all his learning and religious beliefs fit his desire to deceive.

He even seemed to think himself equal to deceiving the Almighty. He would make a short prayer in the morning and a long prayer at night. Strange as it may seem, few men would at times appear more religious than he.

His family prayer meetings always began with singing. But he was a very poor singer himself. Therefore, the duty of starting the hymn generally fell upon me.

He would read his hymn and nod at me to begin. I would at times do so. At others, I would not.

My refusal to obey would almost always produce much confusion. To show he did not need me, he would stagger through the hymn in the most tuneless manner. This was to show himself independent of me. In this state of mind, he prayed with more than ordinary spirit.

Poor man! Such was his **disposition**. And such was his success at deceiving that I truly believe he sometimes deceived himself. He seriously believed that he was a sincere worshipper of the most high God. This, too, when he may be said to have been especially guilty of forcing his woman slave to commit **adultery**.

The facts in the case are these. Mr. Covey was a poor man. He was just starting off in life. So he was only able to buy one slave. Shocking as is the fact, he bought her, as he said, for a *breeder*.[6]

---

[6]"Breeder" is a term for an animal that is kept so it will produce offspring. In the days of slavery, slaves were "bred" very much like cattle.

This woman was named Caroline. Mr. Covey bought her from Thomas Lowe, about six miles from St. Michael's. She was a large, able-bodied woman, about twenty years old. She had already given birth to one child. This proved her to be just what he wanted.

After buying her, Mr. Covey hired a married man to live with him one year. (This man belonged to Mr. Samuel Harrison.) And him Mr. Covey used to fasten up with her every night! The result was that, at the end of the year, the miserable woman gave birth to twins.

At this result, Mr. Covey seemed to be highly pleased with the man and the wretched woman. Such was the Coveys' joy that nothing they could do for Caroline during her confinement[7] was too good or hard to be done. The children were regarded as being quite an addition to his wealth.

If there was one time that was harder than any other, it was during the first six months of my stay with Mr. Covey. During that time, I was made to drink the bitterest **dregs** of slavery.

We were worked in all weathers. It was never too hot or too cold. It could never rain, blow, hail, or snow too hard for us to work in the field.

Work, work, work was scarcely more the order of the day than of the night. The longest days were too short for him. And the shortest nights were too long.

I was somewhat unmanageable when I first went there. But a few months of this discipline tamed me. Mr. Covey succeeded in breaking me.

I was broken in body, soul, and spirit. My natural high spirits were crushed. My intellect wasted away. My disposition to read left me. The cheerful spark that lingered about my eye died. The dark night of slavery closed in upon me. Behold a man changed into a brute!

Sunday was my only leisure time. I spent this under some large tree in a sort of beastlike **stupor**, between sleeping and waking.

[7]Confinement is a period when a pregnant woman stays in bed before and after the birth of her baby.

At times I would rise up. A flash of energetic freedom would dart through my soul. Along with this came a faint beam of hope. But after flickering for a moment, they then vanished. I sank down again, mourning over my wretched condition.

I sometimes felt ready to take my life and that of Covey. But I was prevented by a combination of hope and fear. My sufferings on this plantation seem now like a dream rather than a stern reality.

Our house stood within a few rods of the Chesapeake Bay. Its broad surface was always white with sails from every part of the globe.

Those beautiful vessels robed in purest white were a delightful sight to the eye of freemen. But to me, they were just so many **shrouded** ghosts. They terrified and tormented me with thoughts of my wretched condition.

I have often stood all alone upon the high banks of that noble bay. In the deep stillness of a summer's Sabbath,[8] I watched there with saddened heart and tearful eye. I traced the countless number of sails moving off to the mighty ocean.

The sight of these always affected me powerfully. My thoughts demanded to be spoken. And there, with no audience but the Almighty, I would pour out my soul's complaint. I did this in my crude way, crying out to the moving **multitude** of ships:

"You are loosed from your ropes and are free. I am bound in my chains and am a slave! You move merrily before the gentle wind. I move sadly before the bloody whip!

"You are freedom's swift-winged angels that fly around the world. I am confined in bands of iron!

"O, that I were free! O, that I were on one of your gallant decks and under your protecting wing!

"Alas![9] Between you and me, the muddy waters roll. Go on, go on. O, that I could also go! Could I but swim! If

---

[8]The Sabbath is the seventh day of the week; often a holy day of rest. In Christian cultures, this is usually Sunday.
[9]An expression of sadness or sorrow.

I could fly! O, why was I born a man to be turned into a brute!

"That glad ship is gone. She hides in the dim distance. I am left in the hottest hell of unending slavery.

"O, God save me! God, deliver me! Let me be free! Is there any God?

"Why am I a slave? I will run away. I will not stand it. Get caught or get clear, I'll try it. I might as well die with ague[10] as the fever. I have only one life to lose. I might as well be killed running as die standing.

"Just think of it! One hundred miles straight north and I am free! Try it? Yes! God helping me, I will. It cannot be that I shall live and die a slave.

"I will take to the water. This very bay shall yet bear me to freedom. The steamboats steered in a northeast course from North Point.[11] I will do the same.

"When I get to the head of the bay, I will turn my canoe loose. Then I will walk straight through Delaware to Pennsylvania. When I get there, I shall not be required to have a pass. I can travel without being disturbed. Let but the first chance arrive and—come what will—I am off.

"Meanwhile, I will try to bear up under the yoke. I am not the only slave in the world. Why should I fret? I can bear as much as any of them.

"Besides, I am just a boy. And all boys are bound to someone. It may be that my misery in slavery will only increase my happiness when I get free. There is a better day coming."

Thus I used to think, and thus I used to speak to myself. I was driven almost to madness at one moment. At the next, I was reconciling myself to my wretched lot.

I have already hinted that my life was much worse during the first six months of my stay at Mr. Covey's than in the last six. The events that changed Mr. Covey's treatment of me form an important stage in my humble history.

You have seen how a man was made a slave. You shall

---

[10]A kind of fever often connected with the disease malaria.
[11]North Point overlooks the Chesapeake Bay in the northern part of Maryland.

see how a slave was made a man.

It was one of the hottest days of the month of August 1833. Bill Smith, William Hughes, a slave named Eli, and myself were fanning wheat.[12] Hughes was clearing the fanned wheat from before the fan. Eli was turning, Smith was feeding, and I was carrying wheat to the fan.

The work was simple, requiring strength rather than thinking. Yet to one entirely unused to such work, it came very hard.

About three o'clock of that day, I broke down. My strength failed me. I was seized with a violent aching of the head and extreme dizziness. I trembled in every limb.

Knowing what was coming, I nerved myself up. I felt it would never do to stop work.

I stood as long as I could stagger to the hopper with grain. Then I could stand no longer. I fell and felt as if held down by a great weight. The fan, of course, stopped. Everyone had his own work to do. No one could do the work of the other and have his own go on at the same time.

Mr. Covey was at the house. This was about one hundred yards from the yard where we were fanning. On hearing the fan stop, he left immediately and came to the spot where we were.

He hastily asked what the matter was. Bill answered that I was sick. He added that there was no one to bring wheat to the fan.

I had by this time crawled away to the post and rail fence by which the yard was enclosed. I hoped to find relief by getting out of the sun.

Mr. Covey then asked where I was. He was told by one of the hands. He came to the spot. After looking at me awhile, he asked me what was the matter. I told him as well as I could, for I scarce had strength to speak.

He than gave me a savage kick in the side and told me to get up. I tried to do so. But I fell back in the attempt.

---

[12]Fanning separates the wheat berries from the stalks ("chaff"). The hopper is a funnel-like container where the wheat is poured for fanning.

He gave me another kick and again told me to rise. I again tried and succeeded in gaining my feet. Then I stooped to get the tub with which I was feeding the fan. This effort made me stagger and fall again.

While I was still down, Mr. Covey took up a board of hickory. With it, he gave me a heavy blow upon the head. This made a large wound, and the blood ran freely.

Again he told me to get up. I made no effort to **comply**. I had now made up my mind to let him do his worst.

In a short time after receiving this blow, my head grew better. Mr. Covey had now left me to my fate. At this moment, I made a decision. For the first time, I would go to my master. I would complain and ask his protection.

In order to do this, I must that afternoon walk seven miles. This, under the circumstances, was truly a severe undertaking. I was extremely feeble. The kicks and blows which I had received had hurt me as much as my severe fit of sickness.

However, I watched for my chance. While Covey was looking in an opposite direction, I started for St. Michael's. I succeeded in getting some distance on my way to the woods. But then Covey discovered me. He called after me to come back, threatening what he would do if I did not.

I ignored both his calls and his threats. I made my way to the woods as fast as my weakened state would allow. Thinking he might catch me if I kept to the road, I walked through the woods. I kept far enough from the road to avoid being seen. Yet I stayed near enough to prevent losing my way.

I had not gone far before my little strength again failed me. I could go no farther. I fell down and lay for a considerable time. The blood was still oozing from the wound on my head. For a time I thought I would bleed to death. And I think I would have done so if the blood had not so **matted** my hair as to stop the wound.

I lay there about three quarters of an hour. Then I nerved myself up again and started on my way. I went through marshes and thorns, barefooted and bareheaded. Sometimes

I tore my feet at nearly every step.

It took some five hours to make the seven-mile journey. At last I arrived at master's store.

My appearance would have been enough to affect any but one with a heart of iron. From the crown of my head to my feet, I was covered with blood. My hair was all clotted with dust and blood. My shirt was stiff with blood.

My legs and feet were torn in many places with thorns and covered with blood. I suppose I looked like a man who had escaped a den of wild beasts—barely escaped.

In this state I appeared before my master. I humbly begged him to use his authority for my protection. I told him all that had happened as well as I could.

At times as I spoke, it seemed to affect him. He then walked the floor and sought to **justify** Covey by saying he expected I deserved it.

He asked me what I wanted. To let me get a new home, I told him. I said that if I returned to Mr. Covey, I should live with him just to die with him. I explained that Covey would surely kill me. He was well on his way to doing that already.

Master Thomas made fun of the idea that there was any danger of Mr. Covey's killing me. He said he knew Mr. Covey and he was a good man. Master Thomas could not think of taking me from him. If he did, he would lose the whole year's wages.

He insisted that I belonged to Mr. Covey for one year. I must go back to him, come what might. And I must not trouble him with more stories. Otherwise, he would himself *get hold of me.*

After threatening me thus, he gave me a very large dose of salts.[13] He told me that I might remain in St. Michael's that night since it was quite late. But he said I must be off back to Mr. Covey's early in the morning. And if I did not, he would *get hold of me.* This meant that he would whip me.

I remained all night. According to his orders, I started

---

[13]Salts (such as Epsom salts) are used to clean out the stomach and intestines.

off to Covey's in the morning (Saturday morning). I felt weary in body and broken in spirit.

I reached Covey's about nine o'clock. Just as I was getting over the fence that divided Mrs. Kemp's fields from ours, out ran Covey with his cowskin. He was ready to give me another whipping.

Before he could reach me, I succeeded in getting to the cornfield. As the corn was very high, it gave me the means of hiding.

He seemed very angry and searched for me for a long time. My behavior was altogether **unaccountable**. He finally gave up the chase. I suppose he thought I must come home for something to eat. So he decided to give himself no further trouble in looking for me.

I spent that day mostly in the woods, thinking of the choices before me. I could go home and be whipped to death. Or I could stay in the woods and be starved to death.

That night, I met up with Sandy Jenkins. He was a slave with whom I was somewhat acquainted. Sandy had a free wife who lived about four miles from Mr. Covey's. Since it was Saturday, Sandy was on his way to see her.

I told Sandy my circumstances. He very kindly invited me to go home with him.

I went home with him and talked this whole matter over. I got his advice as to what course it was best for me to pursue. I found Sandy an old adviser. He told me, with great seriousness, I must go back to Covey.

But before I went, I must go with him to another part of the woods. There could be found a certain *root*. He said I should take some of it with me, carrying it *always on my right side*. This would make it impossible for Mr. Covey, or any other white man, to whip me.

Sandy said he had carried the root for years. Since he had done so, he had never received a blow. And he never expected to while he carried it.

At first I rejected the idea. How could the simple carrying of a root in my pocket have any such effect? I did not wish to take it. But with much seriousness, Sandy impressed upon me the necessity. Besides, he told me, even if it did no good, it could do no harm.

To please him, I at length took the root. According to his direction, I carried it upon my right side. This was Sunday morning.

I immediately started for home. Upon entering the yard gate, I met Mr. Covey on his way to church. He spoke to me very kindly. After asking me to drive the pigs from a nearby lot, he passed on toward the church.

Now this strange conduct of Mr. Covey really made me begin to think. Was there something in the *root* which Sandy had given me? If it had been any other day than Sunday, I would have said only the root could explain Mr. Covey's conduct.

As it was, I was half inclined to believe the root was more than I at first had guessed.

All went well till Monday morning. On this morning, the power of the *root* was fully tested. It was long before daylight. I was called to go and rub, curry,[14] and feed the horses. I obeyed and was glad to obey.

I began throwing down some hay from the loft. While I was doing this, Mr. Covey entered the stable with a long rope. Just as I was half out of the loft, he caught hold of my legs. He started tying me.

Soon as I realized what he was up to, I gave a sudden spring. As I did so, he held on to my legs. Thus I was sent sprawling on the stable floor.

Mr. Covey seemed now to think he had me and could do what he pleased. But at this moment, I resolved to fight. Where the spirit came from, I don't know. But suiting my action to my resolution, I seized Covey hard by the throat.

As I did so, I rose. He held on to me, and I to him.

My **resistance** was so entirely unexpected that Covey seemed taken all aback. He trembled like a leaf. This gave me confidence, and I held him uneasily. The blood ran where I touched him with the ends of my fingers.

---

[14]To "curry" means to comb a horse.

Mr. Covey soon called out to Hughes for help, and Hughes came. While Covey held me, Hughes attempted to tie my right hand. As he was in the act of doing so, I watched my chance. I was able to give him a heavy kick close under the ribs.

This kick truly sickened Hughes. He left me in the hands of Mr. Covey.

This kick had the effect of not only weakening Hughes but Covey also. When he saw Hughes bending over with pain, his courage left him. He asked me if I meant to continue with my resistance. I told him I did, come what might. I said he had used me like a brute for six months. Now I was determined to be used so no longer.

With that, Mr. Covey tried to drag me to a stick lying just outside the stable door. He meant to knock me down.

But just as he was leaning over to get the stick, I seized him with both hands by his collar. With a sudden snatch, I brought him to the ground.

By this time, Bill came. Covey called upon him for help. Bill wanted to know what he could do.

Covey said, "Take hold of him! Take hold of him!"

Bill said his master hired him out to work and not to help whip me. So he left Covey and myself to fight our own battle out.

We were at it for nearly two hours. Covey at length let me go, puffing and blowing at a great rate. He said that if I had not resisted, he would not have whipped me half so much.

The truth was that he had not whipped me at all. I considered him as getting entirely the worst end of the bargain. For he had drawn no blood from me, but I had from him.

The whole six months afterwards that I spent with Mr. Covey, he never laid the weight of his finger upon me in anger. He would sometimes say that he didn't want to get hold of me again.

"No," thought I, "you need not. For you will come off worse than you did before."

This battle with Mr. Covey was a turning point in my

career as a slave. It relit a few dying sparks of freedom. It **revived** within me a sense of my own manhood. My departed self-confidence was recalled. And I was inspired again with a determination to be free.

The pleasure this triumph gave me was a full **compensation** for whatever else might follow—even death. Few can know the deep satisfaction which I experienced. Only those who have forcefully pushed away the bloody arm of slavery can understand.

I felt as I never felt before. It was a glorious **resurrection**. I climbed from the tomb of slavery to the heaven of freedom. My long-crushed spirit rose. Cowardice departed, and bold **defiance** took its place.

I now made a resolution. It didn't matter how long I might remain a slave in name. The day had passed forever when I could be a slave in fact. A white man who expected to succeed in whipping must also succeed in killing me. I did not hesitate to let this be known of me.

I remained a slave four years afterward. But from this time, I was never again what might be called really whipped. I had several fights but was never whipped.

It was for a long time a surprise to me why Mr. Covey did not have me taken by the constable[15] to the whipping post. There I would have been regularly whipped for raising my hand against a white man to defend myself.

The only explanation I can now think of does not entirely satisfy me. But such as it is, I will give it.

Mr. Covey enjoyed the most limitless reputation. He was considered a first-rate overseer and negro-breaker. This was of great importance to him.

That reputation was at stake. I was but a boy of about sixteen years old. Had he sent me to the public whipping post, his reputation would have been lost. So, to save his reputation, he allowed me to go unpunished.

---

[15]An old-fashioned term for a police officer.

INSIGHTS INTO
FREDERICK DOUGLASS
(1818?-1895)

Frederick Douglass was christened Frederick Bailey at birth. He changed his last name to Douglass after escaping from slavery. In this way he hoped to avoid being found by his owners.

Douglass had to cope with a number of mysteries about his background. For one thing, like most slaves, he was uncertain of his birth date. At best guess he was probably born in February of 1818.

Douglass also never knew for sure who his father was. Most likely, he was Captain Aaron Anthony, Douglass' master.

When Frederick was a child, his mother was hired out as a field slave. Her employer lived 12 miles away. Just to see her son meant that she had a long trip back each night on foot. Since she had to go to work the next day, the trip was a great physical and emotional strain. She grew ill and died when Douglass was quite young.

Devotion was not the only special thing about Douglass' mother. She was the only slave in Tuckahoe, Maryland, who could read. That fact filled Douglass with great pride. He claimed that his brains came from his mother's side, not his white father's.

continued

Douglass lived with his grandparents until the age of six or seven. At that time he was taken to his master's house. There he discovered what slave life was really like. He was hungry most of the time. In fact, he would hurry after the servant girl to get the bones and crumbs when she shook the tablecloth.

These experiences led Douglass to realize, even as a child, that slavery was unjust.

When he was eight, Douglass was sent to Baltimore to live with Hugh Auld. (Auld was a relative of the Anthonys.) Douglass was so eager to read and write that he begged his mistress to teach him. Mrs. Auld agreed, and Douglass learned quickly.

But then Mrs. Auld made the mistake of telling her husband of Douglass' progress. Hugh Auld ordered that all lessons cease. From then on, Mrs. Auld tried to make sure that Douglass never saw a book or paper.

Despite the Aulds' efforts, Douglass' desire to learn only increased. Believing that knowledge would help set him free, he seized any chance to study. For instance, when he was eleven, Douglass went to work at his master's shipyards. When he could, he practiced writing by imitating the letters on ships.

On September 2, 1838, Douglass ran away to the free state of New York. Then he and his new wife moved to Massachusetts. There Douglass found work in a shipyard.

Though Douglass was on free soil, his past haunted him. He decided to speak out in public against the cruel treatment of slaves.

Naturally this made Douglass enemies. Slavery supporters claimed he was a fraud. They said he'd never been a slave at all.

Douglass responded by publishing a paper. In it he described in detail his life in bondage.

Perhaps unwisely, Douglass used his real name in the paper. Before long, rumors arose that Douglass' owners were after him. Douglass had no choice but to flee to Europe.

When Douglass arrived in Europe, he was stunned by the respect he received. He remarked that he wished Americans were so colorblind.

Douglass spent his time in Europe speaking out against slavery. He earned quite a bit of money from his lectures. But he didn't use it all for himself. He sent most of it to the U.S. to be used in the fight against slavery.

When Douglass had been in Europe for three years, some English friends raised $750 to buy his freedom. Douglass was then able to return to the U.S. in 1847. There he was greeted by his wife and five children.

It had taken almost 30 years, but Douglass was now legally a free man.

Upon his return to the U.S., Douglass set up an anti-slavery newspaper. He was proud of his printing business—the first owned by a black in the U.S.

Douglass wasn't content to rely just on the written word. His emotional speeches against slavery also won many to his side. But many times he walked off the lecture platform wiping egg from his face that angry listeners had thrown.

During the Civil War, Douglass was outraged when he learned black soldiers were paid less than whites. He took his complaint straight to the top by protesting to Lincoln. The President took action at once. He saw to it that the 186,000 blacks in the Union Army were paid just as much as whites.

continued

Even after the Civil War was over, Douglass kept up the fight against prejudice. Two years after his wife died, Douglass married a white woman named Helen Pitts. Both blacks and whites blasted the marriage.

But Douglass defended himself. He explained that he had not abandoned blacks. Instead, by marrying a white woman, he was taking a stand against prejudice.

Other works by Douglass
  Life and Times of Frederick Douglass, book
  My Bondage and My Freedom, book

CIVIL DISOBEDIENCE
HENRY DAVID THOREAU

VOCABULARY PREVIEW

Below is a list of words that appear in the story. Read the list and get to know the words before you start the story.

agents—representatives; servants
allegiance—loyalty; faithfulness
bias—to influence or sway
conscience—sense of right and wrong; moral sense
corrupt—dishonest; crooked
expedient—resource or tool; means to an end
friction—a clashing or grinding
green—easily fooled; inexperienced
immortality—a life without end; deathlessness
imposed (on)—taken advantage of; cheated
indispensable—necessary; called-for
institution—company; organization
legislators—lawmakers; representatives or senators
novel—new; original
occupants—dwellers
offense—fault; crime
on behalf of—representing; acting for
poverty—poorness; neediness
prevail—win or succeed
remedy—medicine or cure

CIVIL DISOBEDIENCE[1]

HENRY DAVID THOREAU

Do we serve the government?

Or should it serve us?

Thoreau is in no doubt:
government should serve us.
And until it serves us better,
we should deny its power.
Even if that means spending
some time in jail.

---

[1] This title was probably not what Thoreau himself intended. It was given to the essay after Thoreau died. When it was first printed in 1849, it was called "Resistance to Civil Government." Civil disobedience is the refusal to obey laws in order to change the government.

I heartily accept the motto: "That government is best which governs least."[2] But I should like to see it acted out more rapidly and thoroughly. Carried out, it finally amounts to this, which I also believe: "That government is best which governs not at all." When men are prepared for it, that will be the kind of government they have.

Government is at best an **expedient**. But most governments are usually—and all governments are sometimes—inexpedient.

Objections have been brought against a standing army.[3] They are many and weighty and deserve to **prevail**. These arguments may also at last be brought against a standing government.

The government itself is only the means which people have chosen to carry out their will. But it is equally likely to be abused and twisted before the people can act through it.

Consider the present Mexican War.[4] This is the work of a few individuals who have used the government as their tool. For at the beginning, the people would not have consented to this war.

What is this American government? It is just a tradition, though a recent one, trying to pass itself along unchanged to posterity. But each instant, it is losing some of its integrity.

The government has not the energy and force of a single living man. A single man can bend it to his will. It is a sort of wooden gun to the people themselves. If they ever use it seriously as a real gun against each other, it will surely split.

But it is no less necessary, even so. The people must have some complicated machinery or other and hear the noise it makes. This satisfies that idea of government which they have.

---

[2] The quote is from John O'Sullivan (1813-1895), an American editor, diplomat, and legislator.

[3] A "standing army" is an army kept in both times of war and peace.

[4] The Mexican War (1846-1848) was not declared by Congress but by President James Polk. In part, the war started because Mexico was angered when the U.S. claimed Texas. (Texas was once part of Mexico.) As a result of the war, the U.S. took over California. Many people of Thoreau's time thought that Polk simply used the war to add land to the U.S. It seems Thoreau shared this view.

Governments show thus how successfully men can be **imposed** on. Men even impose on themselves for their own advantage.

This government is excellent, we must all admit. Yet it never furthered any business except by quickly getting out of the way.

It does not keep the country free. *It* does not settle the West. *It* does not educate. The American people themselves have done all that has been accomplished. They would have done somewhat more if the government had not sometimes gotten in their way.

For government is an expedient by which men try to let one another alone. And, as has been said, it is most expedient when the governed are most let alone by it.

Trade and commerce must be made out of rubber. Otherwise, they would never bounce over the problems which **legislators** continually put in their way.

We judge these legislators partly by their intentions. But what if we were to judge them wholly by the effects of their actions? They would deserve to be classed and punished like mischief-makers who block the railroads.

But I must speak practically and as a citizen. I am not like those who call themselves no-government men. I am not asking all at once for no government. But I ask *at once* for a better government. Let every man make known what kind of government would command his respect. That will be one step toward getting it.

When power is once in the hands of the people, a majority are permitted to rule. And for a long period they continue to do so. But this is not because they are most likely to be in the right. Nor is it because this seems fairest to the minority. It is because they are physically the strongest.

But a government in which the majority rules in all cases cannot be based on justice. Not even justice in the limited way that men understand it.

Can there not be a different kind of government in which majorities do not decide right and wrong? Cannot **conscience** rule instead? So majorities would decide only those questions where expediency is the issue?

Must the citizen ever and even slightly turn over his conscience to the legislator? Why has every man a conscience, then? I think that we should be men first and subjects afterward.

It is not desirable to learn a respect for the law so much as for the right. There is only one duty which I have the obligation to assume. This is to do at any time what I think right.

It is truly enough said that a corporation has no conscience.[5] But a corporation of conscientious men is a corporation *with* a conscience. Law never made men a bit more just. By respecting it, even the well-meaning are daily made the **agents** of injustice.

***

Unjust laws exist. Shall we be content to obey them? Or shall we try to change them and obey them until we have succeeded? Or shall we break them at once?

Under such a government as this, men generally think they ought to wait until persuading the majority to change the laws. They think that if they resist, the **remedy** would be worse than the evil.

But it is the government's fault that the remedy *is* worse than the evil. *It* makes it worse. Why is it not more willing to anticipate and provide for reform? Why does it not value its wise minority? Why does it cry and resist before it is hurt?

Why does it not encourage its citizens to be on the alert to point out its faults? Why does it not *do* better so it would not have faults?

Why does it always crucify Christ? Why does it ban Copernicus and Luther from the church? Why does it declare

---

[5]This statement was made by Sir Edward Coke (1552-1634), an English judge. (A corporation is a business owned by one or more people. By law, the owners are not responsible for the debts of the corporation.)

Washington and Franklin rebels?[6]

What is the only **offense** never dreamed of by a government? One would think that it was the denial of the government's power. Otherwise, why has the government not given that offense a fixed, suitable, and correct penalty?

Suppose a man who has no property refuses but once to earn nine shillings for the State.[7] He is put in prison for a period unlimited by any law that I know. His sentence is left up to those who placed him there.

But suppose he should steal ninety times nine shillings from the State. He is soon permitted to go at large again.

Perhaps injustice is part of the necessary **friction** of the machine of government. If so, let it go, let it go. Maybe it will wear smooth. Certainly the machine will wear out.

Injustice may operate on its own power through a spring, pulley, rope, or crank. If this is the case, perhaps the remedy is not worse than the evil.

But suppose injustice requires you to be the agent of injustice to another. Then, I say, break the law. Let your life serve as friction to stop the machine. What I have to do, at any rate, is see that I do not lend myself to the wrong which I condemn.

As for the ways the State has for remedying evil, I know not of such ways. They take too much time, and a man's life will be gone. I have other business to attend to.

I did not come into this world chiefly to make it a good place to live in. I was born to live in it, be it good or bad.

A man has not everything to do, but something. He cannot possibly do *everything*. Therefore, it is not necessary that he should do *something* wrong.

It is not my business to petition the government or the

---

[6] Jesus was the founder of Christianity. Copernicus was an astronomer and Martin Luther the founder of Protestantism. All three men offended religious leaders of their day. George Washington was a general during the American Revolution and later the first U.S. president. Benjamin Franklin was an author, politician, inventor, and a leader of the American Revolution.

[7] Thoreau is referring to the nine shillings that citizens used to have to pay to vote. (A shilling was a type of coin.) All such poll taxes were finally outlawed in the U.S. in 1966.

legislature any more than it is theirs to petition me. And if they should not hear my petition, what should I do then?

But in this case, the State has provided no way to petition. Its very Constitution is the evil.

This may seem to be harsh and stubborn and unbending. But it actually treats with the greatest kindness and respect the only spirit that can appreciate or deserve it. And all change is for the better, like birth and death, which shake the body.

I do not hesitate to say this to those who call themselves abolitionists.[8] They should at once completely withdraw their support—both in person and property—from the government of Massachusetts.

They should not wait till they are a majority of one before they allow the right to prevail through them. I think that it is enough if they have God on their side without waiting for anyone else. Moreover, any man more right than his neighbors makes a majority of one already.

I meet this American government—or its representative, the State government—just once a year. It comes to me in the person of its tax gatherer. (This is the only way in which a man like me meets it.) It then says distinctly, "Recognize me."

There is a simple and highly effective way of dealing with this issue. In fact, in the present state of things, it is the most **indispensable** way. That is to express your small satisfaction with and love for it and deny it.

My friendly neighbor is a tax gatherer. He is the man I have to deal with. It is, after all, with men and not with paper that I quarrel. And he has chosen to be an agent of the government.

How shall he ever know well what he is? How shall he ever know what he does as an officer of the government? Or as a man?

He shall not know until he must consider whether to treat

[8]Abolitionists wanted to outlaw slavery.

me—his neighbor—as a neighbor and well-meaning man. Or whether he shall treat me as a madman and disturber of the peace, thinking and speaking with a rudeness to match his actions.

I know this well. Let there be one thousand—or even one hundred—*honest* men in the State of Massachusetts. Or ten *honest* men only. Or let just *one* HONEST man—who has *ceased to hold slaves*—withdraw from this partnership with Massachusetts and be jailed. If this happened, it would be the end of slavery in America.

For it matters not how small the beginning may seem to be. What is once well done is done forever.

But we love better to talk about it. We say that is our mission. Reform keeps numerous newspapers in its service, but not one man. . . .

Under a government which imprisons anyone unjustly, the true place for a just man is a prison. This is their proper place today. The only place which Massachusetts has provided for her freer and less despairing spirits is her prisons.

The just men are thus put out or locked out of the State by her own acts. But they have already put themselves out by their principles. It is there that just men should be looked for.

The runaway slave and Mexican prisoner on parole[9] should come there. It is there that the Indian should come to plead the wrongs of his race. There the just men should be found on that separate but more free and honorable ground. There the State places those who are not *with* her but *against* her. It is the only house in a slave state where a free man can live with honor.

Some think that their influence would be lost there. They believe their voices will no longer disturb the ear of the State. They worry that they would not be as an enemy within its walls.

---

[9]Parole is a system where a prisoner is excused from serving the rest of a sentence. In return, he or she must strictly obey the law and special rules.

But they do not know how much stronger truth is than error. Nor how much more movingly and usefully one can combat injustice who has felt a little of it.

Cast your whole vote, not just a strip of paper. Cast your whole influence. A minority is powerless while it conforms to the majority. It is not even a minority then. But it is overpowering when it clogs the machine with its whole weight.

Suppose the State were given a choice. It could keep all just men in prison. Or it could give up war and slavery. The State would not hesitate which to choose.

Suppose a thousand men were not to pay their tax bills this year. That would not be a violent and bloody measure. It would be more so if they paid those bills. That would allow the State to commit violence and shed innocent blood. That is, in fact, the definition of a peaceable revolution, if any is possible.

"But what shall I do?" So might ask the tax gatherer or any other public officer—as one, in fact, has asked me.

My answer is, "If you really wish to do anything, resign your office." When a person refuses **allegiance** and the officer has resigned, then the revolution has succeeded.

But even suppose blood should flow. Is there not a sort of blood shed when the conscience is wounded? Through this wound, a man's real manhood and **immortality** flow out. He bleeds to an everlasting death. I see this blood flowing now.

I have been considering the imprisonment of the offender rather than the seizure of his goods. Both will serve the same purpose. But those who press for the purest justice are the most dangerous to a **corrupt** state. And commonly, they have not spent much time in gathering property.

To them, the State gives small service. Therefore, even a slight tax is likely to appear too great. This is particularly so if they have to earn the money by special labor with their hands.

Suppose there were one who lived wholly without the use of money. The State itself would hesitate to demand it of him. But—not to make an offensive comparison—the rich man is always sold to the **institution** that makes him rich.

Strictly speaking, the more money a man has, the less his virtue. Money comes between a man and his goals and buys them for him. And it was certainly no great virtue that got him money.

Money puts to rest many questions which a man would otherwise be hard pressed to answer. The only new question which it puts is the hard but unimportant one: how to spend it.

Thus a man's moral ground is taken from under his feet. The chances for living decrease as what are called the "means" increase. The best thing a man can do for his culture is to try to carry out those schemes he had when he was poor.

Christ answered the Herodians[10] according to their beliefs. "Show me the tax money," said he. And one took a penny out of his pocket.

So Christ pointed out that they used money which had the image of Caesar on it. It was Caesar who made it accepted and valuable. That is, the Herodians were *men of the State.* So if they enjoyed the advantages of Caesar's government, they should pay back some of his own when he demanded it:

"Give therefore to Caesar that which is Caesar's. And give to God those things which are God's," as Christ said.

This left the Herodians no wiser than before as to which things belonged to which ruler. But, in fact, they did not wish to know.

When I talk with the freest of my neighbors, I see that they speak about the size and seriousness of this issue. They speak freely about their concern for public peace.

But the long and short of the matter is this. They cannot give up the protection of the existing government. And they dread what might happen to their property and families if

---

[10]By "Herodians," Thoreau means those loyal to Herod, the ruler of Israel in Christ's time. Herod was really a puppet of the Roman Emperor Caesar Augustus. The story Thoreau refers to is from the Bible (Matthew 22:16-21), when the Herodians asked Christ if they should pay taxes to Rome.

they disobeyed.

For my own part, I should not like to think that I ever rely on the State's protection. But suppose I deny the State's claim to rule me when it presents its tax bill. It will soon take and waste all my property. And it will bother me and my children without end.

This is hard. This makes it impossible for a man to live both honestly and comfortably in terms of his material life. It will not be worth the while to get more property. It would be sure to be lost again.

You must hire or squat somewhere.[11] You must raise just a small crop—and eat that soon. You must live within yourself and depend upon yourself. You must always be packed up and ready to leave. You must not have many business affairs.

A man may grow rich even in Turkey. But he must be in all respects a good subject of the Turkish government.

Confucius[12] said this: "If a State is governed by the laws of reason, **poverty** and misery are subjects of shame. If a State is not governed by the laws of reason, riches and honors are the subjects of shame."

No, I can afford to refuse allegiance to Massachusetts. I can deny her any right to my property and my life. I can do so until I want her protection . . . or until I am concerned only with earning riches at home by peaceful dealings.

It costs me less in every sense to suffer the penalty of disobedience to the State than to obey. I should feel as if I were worth less in that case.

Some years ago, the State met me **on behalf of** the church. It commanded me to pay a certain amount to go toward the support of a minister. My father attended his preachings, but I never did myself.

"Pay it," it said, "or be locked up in the jail."

I declined to pay. But, unfortunately, another man saw fit to pay it.

---

[11]That is, you must rent land or simply live on it without renting. A squatter lives in a house or on land without right or title.

[12]Confucius (551-478 B.C.) was an ancient Chinese philosopher.

I did not see the reason for this. Why should the schoolmaster be taxed to support the priest? Yet the priest was not taxed to support the schoolmaster?

For I was not the State's schoolmaster.[13] I supported myself by fees willingly given.

I did not see why the lecture hall should not present a tax bill of its own. To my mind, the State as well as the church should back such a demand.

However, I gave in to a request of the officials. I agreed to make some such statement as this in writing: "Let all men know this. I, Henry Thoreau, do not wish to be regarded as a member of any organized society which I have not joined."

This I gave to the town clerk, and he has it. The State thus learned my wish that I did not want to be regarded as a member of that church. And it has never made a similar demand on me since. However, it did say that it must stick to its original belief that first time.

If I had been able to name them, I should then have signed off from all the societies which I never signed on to. But I did not know where to find a complete list.

I have paid no poll tax for six years. I was put into a jail once for this reason for one night. I stood there considering the walls of solid stone. They were two or three feet thick. The door was of wood and iron and a foot thick. An iron grating strained the light.

I could not help being struck with the foolishness of that institution. It treated me as if I were only flesh and blood and bones, to be locked up.

I wondered that it should have decided that this was the best use it could put me to. It had never thought to use my services in some way.

I saw that there was a wall of stone between me and my townsmen. Yet there was a still more difficult one to climb or break through before they could be as free as I was.

I did not for a moment feel confined. The walls seemed

[13]Thoreau regularly gave talks at the Concord Lyceum. (A lyceum is a lecture hall.)

a great waste of stone and mortar.[14] I felt as if I alone of all my townsmen had paid my tax.

They plainly did not know how to treat me. Instead, they behaved like people who are unrefined. In every threat and in every compliment there was a blunder.

They thought that my chief desire was to stand on the other side of that stone wall. I could not but smile to see how carefully they locked the door. My thoughts, after all, followed them out again without stopping or being blocked. And these thoughts were really all that were dangerous.

But they could not reach me, so they decided to punish my body. They acted as boys will who hurt someone's dog if they cannot take out their grudge on his owner.

I saw that the State was half-witted. It was as fearful as a lone woman with her silver spoons. It did not know its friends from its foes. I lost all my remaining respect for it and pitied it.

Thus the State never tries to deal with a man's sense, intellectual or moral. It deals only with his body, his senses. It is not armed with more wit or honesty but with more physical strength alone.

I was not born to be forced. I will breathe in my own way. Let us see who is the strongest. What force has a crowd? Only those who obey a higher law than I can force me. They force me to become like themselves.

I do not hear of *men* being *forced* to live this way or that by masses of men. What sort of life would that be?

Suppose I meet a government which says to me, "Your money or your life." Why should I be in haste to give it my money? It may be in great difficulties and not know what to do. I cannot help that. It must help itself; do as I do. It is not worth the while to whine about it. I am not responsible for the successful working of the machinery of society. I am not the son of the engineer.

I see what happens when an acorn and a chestnut fall side by side. The one does not remain lifeless to make way for

---

[14]Mortar is a cementlike mixture used to hold bricks or stones together.

the other. Both obey their own laws and spring and grow as best they can. They do so till one, perhaps, overshadows and destroys the other.

If a plant cannot live according to its nature, it dies. So does a man.

That night in prison was **novel** and interesting enough. The prisoners were in shirtsleeves. They were enjoying a chat and the evening air in the doorway when I entered.

But the jailer said, "Come, boys, it is time to lock up." And so they split up. I heard the sound of their steps returning to the hollow cells.

My roommate was introduced to me by the jailer as "a first-rate fellow and an honest man." When the door was locked, he showed me where to hang my hat and how he managed matters there.

The rooms were whitewashed once a month. This one, at least, was the whitest, neatest, and most simply furnished room in town.

He naturally wanted to know where I came from and what brought me there. When I told him, I asked him in my turn what brought him there. I assumed he was an honest man, of course. And as the world goes, I believe he was.

"Why," said he, "they accused me of burning a barn. But I never did it."

As near as I could discover, he had probably gone to bed in a barn when drunk. He smoked his pipe there, and so a barn was burnt.

He had the reputation of being an honest man. He had been there some three months waiting for his trial to come on. And he would have to wait at least another three months.

But he was quite at home and happy. After all, he got his board[15] for nothing. He thought he was well treated.

He occupied one window, and I the other. I saw that if one stayed there long, one's main business would be to look out the window.

---

[15]Board is food supplied every day, usually in return for money or work.

I had soon read all the tracts[16] that were left there. I examined where former prisoners had broken out and where a grate had been sawed off. And I heard the history of the various **occupants** of that room. I found that even here there was history and gossip, though it never went beyond the jail walls.

Verses were written there and passed along to everybody. But this was probably the only house in the town where they were not published.

I was shown quite a long list of verses. These were written by some young men who had been caught in an attempt to escape. They got revenge by singing them.

I pumped my fellow prisoner as dry as I could. I was afraid I should never see him again. But at length, he showed me which was my bed and left me to blow out the lamp.

To lie there that night was like traveling into a far country—a place such as I had never expected to see. It seemed to me that I never had heard the town clock strike before. Or that I had ever heard the evening sounds of the village. For we slept with the windows open, which were inside the grating.

It was like seeing my village in the light of the Middle Ages.[17] And our Concord was turned into a Rhine stream. Visions of knights and castles passed before me. There were voices of ancient villagers that I heard in the streets.

Whether I wanted to or not, I heard what was done and said in the kitchen of the nearby village inn. This was a wholly new and rare experience to me.

It was a closer view of my native town. I was actually inside of it. I had never seen its institutions before. This jail was one of its unique institutions, for the village is a county seat. I began to understand what its people were about.

In the morning, our breakfasts were put through the hole

---

[16]In this case, tracts are religious booklets.
[17]The Middle Ages was a period between the 5th and 15th centuries. It was a period known for heroism, knights, and castles. Concord is the name of both the Massachusetts town Thoreau lived in and the river which ran through it. The Rhine is a river in Western Europe, famous in many legends.

in the door. They were in small rectangular tin pans, made to fit. They held a pint of chocolate with brown bread and an iron spoon.

When they called for the pans again, I was **green** enough to return what bread I had left. But my roommate seized it. He said I should save it for lunch or dinner.

Soon after, he was let out to work. Every day he went haying in a neighboring field. He would not be back till noon. So he said good-day to me, saying he doubted if he should see me again.

Then someone interfered and paid the tax. So I came out of prison.

I did not see that great changes had taken place on the common.[18] It was not as if I had gone in as a youth and then come out as a tottering and gray-headed man.

And yet to my eyes, a change had come over the scene— the town, State, and country. It was a greater change than any that only time could make.

I saw yet more clearly the State in which I lived. I saw to what extent the people among whom I lived could be trusted as good neighbors and friends. I realized that their friendship was for summer weather only.

They did not greatly wish to do right. They were of a different race from me because of their prejudices and superstitions. They were as different from me as the Chinamen and Malays are.[19]

I also saw that they might make sacrifices to humanity. But they ran no risks, not even to their property. They were not so noble after all. They treated the thief as he had treated them. They hoped to save their souls with an outward show and a few prayers. They would walk a straight though useless path from time to time.

Perhaps I am judging my neighbors harshly. I believe that most are not aware that they have such an institution as the jail in their village.

---

[18]A common is a public square or park in the center of a town.
[19]Malays are from Malaysia, a country in southeast Asia.

There was once a custom in our village. When a poor debtor came out of jail, his friends would greet him by looking through their fingers. These were crossed to represent the grating of a jail window. "How do ye do?" they would say.

My neighbors did not greet me this way. Instead, they first looked at me and then at one another. They acted as if I had returned from a long journey.

I had been put into jail as I was going to the shoemaker's to get a mended shoe. So when I was let out the next morning, I went on to finish my errand.

Having put on my mended shoe, I joined a huckleberry-picking party. They were impatient to put themselves under my leadership.

The horse was soon harnessed. And in half an hour, I was in the midst of the huckleberry field on one of our highest hills, two miles off. From there, the State was nowhere to be seen.

This is the whole history of "My Prisons."[20]

I have never declined to pay the highway tax. That is because I wish to be a good neighbor as much as a bad subject. I also believe in supporting schools. I am doing my part to educate my fellow countrymen now.

Why, then, do I refuse to pay the tax bill? It is for no particular item that I refuse to pay taxes. I simply wish to refuse allegiance to the State. I want to withdraw and stand away from it completely.

Even if I could, I do not care to track the path of my dollar. Not until it buys a man—or a musket to shoot me with. After all, the dollar is innocent. But I am concerned with tracing the effects of my allegiance.

In fact, I quietly declare war with the State in my own way. But I will still make use and get from her whatever advantage I can, as is usual in such cases.

Others may pay the tax for me from a sympathy with the

---

[20]*My Prisons* (1832) was a book by Italian poet and playwright Silvio Pelico (1789-1854). Pelico suffered in prison for many years. Thoreau refers to the book to jokingly remind us that he only spent one night in jail.

State. But in paying the tax, they do what they have already done in their own case. Or rather they do more to aid injustice than the State requires.

Perhaps they pay the tax from a mistaken interest in the individual taxed. They want to save his property or prevent his going to jail. But if they do this, they have not thought wisely enough. They let their private feelings interfere with the public good.

This, then, is my position at present. But one cannot be too much on his guard in such a case. Otherwise, one might let stubbornness or regard for the opinions of others **bias** him. Let a man make sure that he does only what is right for himself and for the moment.

INSIGHTS INTO
HENRY DAVID THOREAU
(1817-1862)

Henry David Thoreau lived at a time when most writers were wealthy and well-educated. But Thoreau's family was far from rich. His mother took in boarders, and his father had a shop where he made pencils.

Thoreau's insights helped the family somewhat. To improve his father's business, he studied European pencil-making methods. He came back from his research with ways to make pencils better than any produced in America. Because of his efforts, the family business thrived.

For a time Thoreau made his living as a teacher. However, his teaching methods were too forward-looking to please the school. He was also criticized for refusing to physically punish his students.

Thoreau soon quit this job and opened his own school with his brother John. There he had things his way. His school offered outdoor classes. There was no physical punishment. And subjects were related to real life.

When John died of lockjaw, a grieving Henry closed the school. For a while he was Concord's jack-of-all-trades. He worked at everything from building barns to milking cows. Then his friend Ralph Waldo Emerson invited Thoreau to move in with the Emersons. For room and board, he worked as handyman and companion to Emerson's children.

continued

Thoreau was friends with many other famous writers of his day. One of them was Nathaniel Hawthorne, author of *The Scarlet Letter.* Hawthorne was a great admirer and helped make Thoreau well known in England.

Horace Greeley, editor of the *New York Tribune,* was another fan. He thought so much of Thoreau's writing that he acted as his agent for free.

Thoreau was always interested in natural history and science. Therefore, when Emerson bought a wooded lot on Walden Pond, Thoreau asked to build a cabin there. He wanted to make his life simpler and lower his cost of living. He also hoped to study nature and spend time writing.

Emerson granted the request. So with a borrowed ax, Thoreau soon built his home on the pond's edge. He lived in the cabin for two years, two months, and two days.

While living on Walden Pond, Thoreau finished several books. However, he couldn't get his first effort, *A Week on the Concord and Merrimack Rivers,* published. After two years of rejection slips, he agreed to pay the cost of publishing the book himself.

Sadly, the book was a complete failure. It took Thoreau five more years to convince a publisher to accept his book *Walden.* This time Thoreau had a winner. Though sales were slow at first, the book grew more popular as time passed. Except for a few years between the first and second printings, the book has never gone out of print.

What happened to the cabin at Walden Pond? For a while, it was home to Emerson's gardener. Then the house was moved across Concord, and the roof was used to cover a pig pen. The rest of the house was used to repair a barn. Doubtless Thoreau would have been pleased to know his cabin had been put to good use.

Thoreau's interest in observing was once greater than his love of nature. On a fishing trip he and a friend accidentally set the woods afire with their campfire.

Thoreau ran for help. But then instead of aiding the townspeople, he climbed a hill and watched the blaze. As he wrote in his journal, "It was a glorious spectacle, and I was the only one there to enjoy it."

The people of Concord were more practical minded. They were upset with Thoreau. Some even talked about charging him with a crime.

Although Thoreau once fell in love and even proposed marriage, he remained single. This man who loved peace and quiet probably had no room in his life for a partner.

Thoreau died at the age of 44. While studying tree growth, he caught a cold which developed into tuberculosis. The disease was probably worsened by Thoreau's pencil-making business. Years of living with graphite dust had weakened his lungs.

Although he knew he was dying, Thoreau remained cheerful. He continued to visit with neighbors and friends. At one point he was asked if he had made his peace with God. He replied, "I did not know that we had ever quarreled."

Other works by Thoreau
  Cape Cod, book
  The Maine Woods, book
  Walden, book
  A Week on the Concord and Merrimack Rivers, book
  A Yankee in Canada, book

A CUB-PILOT'S EXPERIENCE

MARK TWAIN
from *LIFE ON THE MISSISSIPPI*

VOCABULARY PREVIEW

Below is a list of words that appear in the story. Read the list and get to know the words before you start the story.

adjectives—descriptive words
churn—whip; stir
cramped—limited; crowded
gilded—gold-coated; golden
gruff—harsh; grumpy
imminent—about to occur; approaching
inlaid—decorated with material sunken into a surface
margin—border; edge
memorandum—note; message
mimicking—imitating; copying
pomp—splendor; glory
prudence—caution; carefulness
romantic—heroic; adventurous
serene—calm; peaceful
short—rude; sour
siege—blockade or attack
trifle—a bit; a touch
unpicturesque—ordinary or unimpressive
upholstered—covered; outfitted
vengeful—unforgiving; spiteful

A CUB-PILOT'S EXPERIENCE

MARK TWAIN

*Imagine piloting a
grand old boat up a
grand old river. Imagine
the power of knowing
how to back that boat
out of the smallest
space. Imagine being admired
by friends as you stand
at the wheel.
Then imagine all the
training you'd need to
make that dream come
true!*

The boat was lying on the rocks for four days at
Louisville. There were some other delays. What with all that,
the poor old *Paul Jones* fooled away about two weeks on
the voyage from Cincinnati to New Orleans.

This gave me a chance to get to know one of the pilots. He taught me how to steer the boat. This made the fascination of river life stronger than ever for me.

It also gave me a chance to get to know a young man who had taken deck passage.[1] That's a pity—for he easily borrowed six dollars from me. He promised to return to the boat and pay it back the day after we arrived.

But he probably died or forgot, for he never came. It was probably the first reason. After all, he had said his parents were wealthy. He explained that he only traveled deck passage because it was cooler.

I soon discovered two things. One was that no ship would soon sail for the Amazon.[2] In fact, not for another ten or twelve years. The other was that the nine or ten dollars in my pocket were not enough for the impossible trip I had planned. This was true even if I could afford to wait for a ship.

Therefore, it followed that I had to come up with a new career. The *Paul Jones* was now bound for St. Louis. I planned a **siege** against my pilot.

At the end of three hard days, he surrendered. He agreed to teach me the Mississippi River[3] from New Orleans to St. Louis. It would cost me five hundred dollars. This would be paid out of the first wages I received after graduating.

So I started the little job of "learning" twelve or thirteen hundred miles of the great Mississippi River. And I did it with all the easy confidence of a person my age.

But I did not really know what I had taken on. If I had, I would not have had the courage to begin. I supposed that all a pilot had to do was to keep his boat in the river. I did not consider that much of a trick since the river was so wide.

The boat backed out from New Orleans at four in the afternoon. It was "our watch"[4] until eight. Mr. Bixby, my

---

[1]Those who took deck passage were the lowest-paying passengers.
[2]The Amazon is a large river in South America.
[3]The Mississippi flows through the United States from Minnesota to the Gulf of Mexico.
[4]A watch is a period of duty.

chief, "straightened her up." He plowed her along past the sterns of the other boats that were at the levee.[5]

Then he said, "Here, take her. Shave those steamships[6] as close as you'd peel an apple."

I took the wheel. My heartbeat fluttered up into the hundreds. We were so close. It seemed to me that we were about to scrape the side off every ship in the line.

I held my breath. And I began to steer the boat away from the danger. I had my own opinion of the pilot who had gotten us into such danger. But I was too wise to express it.

In half a minute, I had a wide **margin** of safety between the *Paul Jones* and the ships. Within ten seconds more, I was pushed aside in disgrace. Mr. Bixby was going into danger again. And he was skinning me alive with criticism for being a coward.

I was stung. But I had to admire the easy confidence of my chief. He loafed from side to side at his wheel. Yet he passed ships so closely that disaster seemed **imminent**.

When he cooled down a little, he told me that the easy passage was near shore. The current was strong away from the shore. Therefore, going upstream, we must hug the bank to go the easy way. Going downstream, we must stay well out in the river to catch the current.

In my own mind, I decided to be a downstream pilot. I would leave the upstreaming to people dead to **prudence**.

Now and then Mr. Bixby called my attention to certain things. He said, "This is Six-Mile Point." I agreed. It was nice enough information, but I could not see the use of it. I was not aware that it was of any interest to me.

Another time he said, "This is Nine-Mile Point." Later he said, "This is Twelve-Mile Point."

They were all about level with the water's edge. To me, they all looked alike. They were boringly **unpicturesque**.

---

[5]The stern is the back of the ship (the bow is the front). A levee is a bank built to keep the river from flooding nearby land.

[6]Steamships were driven by steam power. To make the steam, water was heated in large boilers with a coal or wood fire.

I hoped Mr. Bixby would change the subject. But no, he would steer around a point, hugging the shore with affection. Then he would say, "The calm water ends here. Just by this bunch of China trees. Now we cross over." So he crossed over.

He gave me the wheel once or twice. But I had no luck. I would nearly chip off the edge of a sugar plantation. Or I would turn off course too far from shore. So I dropped back into disgrace and got scolded.

The watch was ended at last. We ate supper and went to bed.

At midnight, the glare of a lantern shone in my eyes. The night watchman said, "Come, get up!"

And then he left. I could not understand this amazing event. So I soon gave up trying to and dozed off to sleep.

Pretty soon the watchman was back again. This time he was **gruff**.

I was annoyed. I said, "Why do you want to bother me in the middle of the night? Now, like as not, I'll not get to sleep again tonight."

The watchman said, "Well if this ain't good, I'm blessed."

The "off-watch" was just turning in. I heard some rough laughter from them. They made such remarks as:

"Hello watchman! Ain't the new cub turned out yet?"

"He's delicate, likely."

"Give him some sugar in a rag.'"[7]

"Send for the maid to sing 'Rock-a-by Baby' to him."

About this time, Mr. Bixby appeared on the scene. Something like a minute later, I was climbing the pilothouse steps. I had some of my clothes on and the rest in my arms. Mr. Bixby was close behind, commenting.

Here was something new—this getting up in the middle of the night to work. It was a detail in piloting that had never occurred to me at all. I knew that boats ran all night.

---

[7]Babies used to be given sugar lumps in a rag to suck on to keep them quiet and calm.

But somehow, I never thought that somebody had to get out of a warm bed to run them.

I began to fear that piloting was not as **romantic** as I had imagined. There was something very real and worklike about this new part of it.

It was a rather cloudy night. However, a fair number of stars were out. The big mate[8] was at the wheel. He had the old tub pointed at a star. And he was holding her straight up the middle of the river.

The shores on either hand were not much more than half a mile apart. But they seemed wonderfully far away. They were ever so vague and dim.

The mate said, "We've got to land at Jones' plantation, sir."

The **vengeful** spirit in me was happy. I said to myself, "I hope you enjoy your job, Mr. Bixby. You'll have a good time finding Mr. Jones' plantation on a night like this. And I hope you never *will* find it as long as you live."

Mr. Bixby said to the mate, "Upper end of the plantation or the lower?"

"Upper."

"I can't do it. The stumps there are out of the water at this stage. It's no great distance to the lower. So you'll have to get along with that."

"All right, sir. If Jones don't like it, he'll have to lump it, I reckon."

And then the mate left. My joy began to cool and my wonder grew. Here was a man who planned to find this plantation on such a night. Not only that, he would find either end of it you wanted.

I really wanted to ask a question. But I was carrying about as many **short** answers as my cargo space could hold. So I held my peace.

All I wanted to ask Mr. Bixby was this. Was he ass enough to really imagine he was going to find that plantation? On a night when all plantations were exactly alike? And all the

[8]A mate is an officer on a ship.

same color?

But I held it in. I used to have fine flashes of prudence in those days.

Mr. Bixby made for the shore. Soon he was scraping it, just as if it had been daylight. And not only that, he was singing:

"Father in heaven, the day is declining," etc.

I thought I had put my life in the hands of a very reckless outcast.

Soon he turned to me and said, "What's the name of the first point above New Orleans?"

I was glad to be able to answer quickly, and I did. I said I didn't know.

"Don't *know?*"

His manner shook me. I was down at the bottom again. But I had to say just what I had said before.

"Well, you're a smart one!" said Mr. Bixby. "What's the name of the *next* point?"

Once more, I didn't know.

"Well, this beats anything. Tell me the name of *any* point or place I told you."

I thought awhile and decided that I couldn't.

"Look here! What do you start out from, above Twelve-Mile Point, to cross over?"

"I—I—don't know."

"You—you—don't know?" he said, **mimicking** my slow manner of speech. "What *do* you know?"

"I—I—nothing, for certain."

"By the great Caesar's ghost,⁹ I believe you! You're the stupidest fool I ever saw or ever heard of. So help me, Moses!¹⁰ The idea of *you* being a pilot—*you*! Why, you don't know enough to pilot a cow down a lane."

⁹Julius Caesar (100-44 B.C.) was an ancient Roman general and ruler. "By great Caesar's ghost" is an expression of outrage and surprise.
¹⁰In the Bible, Moses was a Hebrew leader and prophet. "So help me, Moses" is another expression of outrage or surprise.

Oh, but he was mad! He was a nervous man. So he shuffled from one side of his wheel to the other as if the floor was hot. He would boil awhile to himself. Then he would overflow and scald me again.

"Look here! What do you suppose I told you the names of those points for?"

Shaking, I considered a moment. Then the devil of temptation made me say, "Well, to—to—be entertaining, I thought."

That was a red flag to the bull. He raged and stormed so that I thought it made him blind. He was crossing the river at the time and ran over a trading scow's[11] oar.

Of course, the traders sent up a round of red-hot curses. Never was a man so grateful as Mr. Bixby was. You see, he was full up to the brim. And here were people who could *talk back*.

He threw open a window and thrust his head out. Such an outburst followed as I never heard before. The farther away the scowmen's curses drifted, the higher Mr. Bixby lifted his voice. And the heavier his **adjectives** grew.

When he closed the window, he was empty. You could have drawn a fishing net through him and not caught enough curses to disturb your mother.

Soon he spoke to me in the gentlest way. "My boy, you must get a little **memorandum** book. Every time I tell you a thing, put it down right away. There's only one way to be a pilot. And that is to get this entire river by heart. You have to know it just like ABC."

That was a sad thought for me. My memory was never loaded with anything but blank bullets.

However, I did not feel discouraged long. I judged it was best not to take it all too seriously. Doubtless, Mr. Bixby was "stretching" things some.

Soon he pulled a rope and struck a few strokes on the big bell. The stars were all gone now. The night was as black

---

[11]A scow is a large, flat-bottomed boat. It is used for carrying heavy loads.

as ink. I could hear the wheels **churn** along the bank. I was not certain that I could see the shore.

The voice of the watchman came up the hurricane deck. "What's this, sir?"

"Jones' plantation."

I said to myself, "I wish I might offer a small bet that it isn't." But I did not chirp. I only waited to see.

Mr. Bixby handled the engine bells. In due time, the boat's nose came to the land. A torch glowed from the forecastle.[12] A man skipped ashore.

The darky's voice on the bank said, "Gimme de k'yarpetbag, Mass' Jones."[13]

The next moment, we were going up the river again. All was **serene**.

I thought deeply awhile. Then I said—but not aloud— "Well, finding that plantation was the luckiest accident that ever happened. But it couldn't happen again in a hundred years." And I fully believed it *was* an accident, too.

By the time we had gone seven or eight hundred miles, I was a fairly daring upstream steersman. In daylight, that is. Before we reached St. Louis, I had made a **trifle** of progress in night work. But only a trifle.

I had a notebook. It almost bristled with the names of towns, points, bars, islands, bends, and reaches.[14] But that information was to be found only in the notebook. None of it was in my head.

It made my heart ache to think that I only had half of the river down in my notes. You see, our watch was four hours off and four hours on. There was a long, four-hour gap in my book for every time I slept.

My chief was soon hired to go on a big New Orleans boat. So I packed my bag and went with him.

She was a grand affair. Standing in her pilothouse, I was

---

[12]The forecastle is the upper deck at the front of a ship. The sailors' rooms are there.
[13]"Darky" was a 19th-century slang term for a black person. In dialect, the man is saying, "Give me the carpet bag, Master Jones."
[14]Here a "reach" means a stretch of water.

so high above the water that I seemed perched on a mountain. Her decks stretched far away, fore and aft,[15] below me. I wondered how I could ever have thought the little *Paul Jones* was large.

There were other differences, too. The *Paul Jones'* pilothouse was a cheap, dirty, battered rattletrap. It was **cramped** for room. But here was a rich glass temple. There was room enough to have a dance in here.

It had showy red and gold window curtains. There was a grand sofa with leather cushions, too. And the bench where visiting pilots sat had a back on it. There they would spin yarns and "look at the river."

No wide wooden box filled with sawdust aboard this ship. Instead, they used bright, fanciful cuspidors.[16] There was a nice new oilcloth[17] on the floor, as well. And a big, pleasant stove for winter.

The wheel, with its costly **inlaid** work, stood as high as my head. There were also a wire tiller-rope[18] and bright brass knobs for the bells.

And a tidy, white-aproned, black "texas-tender"[19] was there to serve us. He would bring up tarts, ices, and coffee during the watch. Day and night.

Now this was something like I expected! So I began to take heart. I once more believed that piloting was a romantic sort of job, after all.

The moment we were under way, I began to prowl around the great steamer. I took it all in, filling myself with joy. She was as clean and dainty as a parlor.

Looking down her long, **gilded** saloon[20] was like gazing through a splendid tunnel. An oil painting by some gifted sign painter was on every stateroom[21] door. She glittered

---

[15]"Fore" refers to the front part of the ship. "Aft" refers to the back.

[16]A cuspidor is a container where tobacco chewers spit tobacco juice.

[17]This is a type of waterproof cloth used to protect floors, etc.

[18]A tiller is a device that helps turn the ship.

[19]The rooms for the officers were called "texas" because they were the largest on ship. A "texas-tender" was an officer's servant.

[20]A saloon is a large room where drinks are served.

[21]A stateroom is a private cabin on a ship.

with endless prism-fringed[22] lights.

The clerk's office was elegant. The bar was marvelous. The barkeeper had been barbered and **upholstered** at incredible cost.

The boiler-deck (the second story of the boat, so to speak) was as roomy as a church. Or so it seemed to me.

So was the forecastle. There was no small handful of deckhands, firemen,[23] and workers. In fact, there was a whole army of men down there.

The fires were fiercely glaring from a long row of furnaces. Over them were eight huge boilers! This was fantastic **pomp**.

The mighty engines—but enough of this. I had never felt so fine before. And when a whole host of stylish servants called me "sir," my satisfaction was complete.

---

[22]A prism is a glass object which breaks white light up into the colors of the rainbow.
[23]The firemen are workers who feed the boilers of the steamship to give the ship power.